Books by Joel Friedlander

Body Types:
The Enneagram of Essence Types

A Self-Publisher's Companion:
Expert Advice for Authors Who Want to Publish from
TheBookDesigner.com

The Book Blueprint:
Expert Advice for Creating Industry-Standard Print
Books

(with Betty Sargent)
The Self-Publisher's Ultimate Resource Guide:
Every Indie Author's Essential Directory to Help You
Prepare, Publish, and Promote Professional Looking Books

*28 Ways to Unlock the Pleasures and
Avoid the Pitfalls of Your Creative Life*

Joel Friedlander

Marin Bookworks
SAN RAFAEL, CA

Copyright © 2022 by Joel Friedlander

All rights reserved. No part of this publication may be reproduced, distributed, or transmitted in any form or by any means, including photocopying, recording, or other electronic or mechanical methods, without the prior written permission of the publisher, except in the case of brief quotations embodied in critical reviews and certain other noncommercial uses permitted by copyright law.

Marin Bookworks
San Rafael, CA 94901

Printed in the United States of America

ISBN 978-0-936385-46-4 - Trade paper
ISBN 978-0-936385-47-1 - eBook

First Edition

Copyediting: PeopleSpeak
Cover design: Bookfly Design
Book design: Marin Bookworks
Book production: Ruth Schwartz, aka The Wonderlady

To the creative spirit in you

Dear Reader,

Joel Friedlander wrote this book
before he passed away on May 7th 2021
and didn't have the ability to bring it to print.

I had promised Joel I would arrange
for *Meeting the Muse* to be available
in trade paper and Kindle editions.

I reached out to a good friend of Joel's
in the book publishing industry,
Ruth Schwartz, aka The Wonderlady,
for help. If it wasn't for Ruth stepping in
to do all the publishing work needed,
it would never have seen the light of day.

I also want to thank Patrick Troccolo,
Joel's dearest and oldest friend,
for supporting the costs of bringing
this book to fruition.

With Love and gratitude for having spent
36 years married to Joel,

Jill Friedlander

Contents

Introduction—Creativity and You 1
1. You Are Absolutely Unique 13
2. No One Else Can See What You See 16
3. Other People May Not Understand 20
4. Avoid Taking Credit for Your Good Ideas 23
5. "Never Be the Only One" 27
6. Let What You've Created Speak for Itself 31
7. Believe in Your Work 35
8. Put Yourself into Everything You Produce 38
9. Learn When to Share an Idea 44
10. Don't Let *Perfect* Become the Enemy of *Good* 48
11. Overcome Your Own Resistance 52
12. Say Yes to Your Own Creative Time 56
13. Be Present during the Process of Creation 61
14. Creativity Can Involve Action—or Not 67
15. Tools Have Never Created Anything 71
16. Inspiration Is Beautiful but Overrated 77
17. Creativity Rarely Looks the Way You Think It Will 81

Contents

18. Nothing Is More Common Than a Good Idea	85
19. Taking Steps to Achieve Your Vision Is What Sets You Apart	89
20. What Stimulates Your Creativity?	94
21. You Have an Unending Stream of Creativity	99
22. Embrace Your Muse	103
23. Everything Has a Natural History	108
24. Creativity Can Flourish in Both Freedom and Constraint	115
25. Telling the Winners from the Losers Can Take a Long Time	119
26. Consider Your Life and Death	123
27. Quiet Your Mind	128
28. Don't Dictate to Your Creativity	133
Conclusion—Go and Create	137
Flex-Your-Creativity Exercises	139
Pay Attention	140
Practice Freewriting	143
Create a List of Lists	147
Write a Haiku	151
Take a Walk	153
Establish a Daily Creative Practice	155
Harness Your Moods	157
Brainstorm: Mind Mapping	159
Write a Letter to the Muse	163
Notes	165
About the Author	167

Acknowledgments

This book, and the experiences that went into it, would not have been possible without the incredible love and support I've received from many people over the years, and I'm grateful to have this occasion to acknowledge that help. With thanks to my wife Jill, Roy and Mary Friedlander, Max and Kate, Sharon Goldinger, Adina Cucicov, Michelle Leifer, Randy Cherner, Michael Hoffman, Felix Morrow, George Gurdjieff, Sandra Lee Dennis, Suzanne Murray, Colin Relph, Tom Millea, Gary Rosenthal, Patrick and Susan Troccolo, and my many friends at the Bay Area Independent Publishers Association.

Introduction
Creativity and You

A COUPLE OF MONTHS ago, I happened to take a long look through my Twitter feed. One tweet caught my eye: "18 Ways to Think about Creativity," it said, with a link. I was intrigued, and something perked up inside me when I saw it.

Was it because creativity has been a favorite subject of mine for many years, or was something deeper at work? Was it *coincidence*, *synchronicity*, or *accident*? These—as well as other seemingly unexplainable occurrences—are celebrated in the creative world because they generate unusual discoveries and world-changing insights. They are the chance meetings on a train, the accident of a book falling open at just the right moment.

Seemingly unrelated events, happening at the same time, can lead to new connections. But what makes these apparently random incidents appear to contain meaning remains a mystery.

In any event, I clicked the link to see what the article was all about.

Imagine my surprise when, as the page started to load, I recognized TheBookDesigner.com—my own website.

Yes, it turned out *I* had written this article in 2010 and published it on my blog. At the time it evoked little response, and like many other articles I wrote back then, I put it out of my mind to start working on another article for the following day. In other words, I promptly forgot about it.

And yet, there I was, looking at something I hadn't seen in years. I started to read through the article. There wasn't a lot of content, just a list of one-sentence bullet points.

Many of the thoughts still rang true, years later. A few surprised me: *Did I write that?* The article wasn't bad, but it was very abbreviated, each statement barely able to make its point before I moved on to the next one.

At the time I wrote the article, my blog was in its early days. I had planned to increase the number of visitors quickly by posting a lot of articles. Since I had come

Meeting the Muse

to blogging late in life, I felt I didn't have the leisure to write once a week, like lots of other bloggers did.

No, I wanted to grow my audience quickly. I wanted to make an impact with my work, and I knew I would need a lot of readers to accomplish my goal. I hit on a plan to post articles to my blog *almost every day*.

I wrote and published a new article every weekday. Then I started posting on Sundays, too, by assembling links to posts by other bloggers in my field. For a while, I even posted on Saturdays by writing "off-topic" articles, ones with no connection to independent publishing—the main subject of my blog.

I soon realized that I needed to step up my writing and organizing skills to keep creating all those articles.

I wouldn't recommend you do what I did; it was a brutal schedule, especially for a newcomer. On many days, the biggest challenge I faced was thinking of something new to write about. Late at night, I sometimes found myself staring blankly at my screen, wondering what to do, or surfing the web for inspiration.

One of the ironies I learned about blogging early on was this: how people responded to my articles bore no relation to the work and effort I had put into them. Articles I spent days researching, writing, and carefully editing often got little or no response.

Others, dashed off in the dark hours to beat my midnight deadline, would instantly attract comments and stimulate conversation. (This isn't very different from what big publishers experience, by the way. Their lists of new books always contain winners and losers. The problem is, no one knows which is which until they are published.)

And so it was with this little post on creativity.

Freewriting

In the two years before I started blogging, I wrote daily in a *freewriting* practice and once a week with a freewriting group led by writer and poet Suzanne Murray. Freewriting involves using a writing prompt and writing faster than you can think for a set amount of time. You write *without interruption* as fast as you can until the timer rings. Then you stop. (You can find more information on freewriting in the exercise section of this book.)

This way of writing changed me, and it changed my life.

Freewriting reestablished my connection with my creative source. I had spent many years writing only business-related copy, such as promotional ads, fundraising letters, and annual reports, all impersonal from the writer's point of view.

Meeting the Muse

Since my college days I had wanted to be a writer. I learned to see the world as an observer of life and dreamed, like all young writers do, of making an impression with my work. I was held back by my inability to find a style of my own, a voice that wasn't an imitation of someone else. I had no confidence in myself, and the urge to write was stymied by my own misgivings.

Eventually, I stopped writing altogether.

By the time I started Suzanne's class, I had become what she called a "crushed creative." Freewriting freed me from the prison I had created for myself.

As I got better at the very simple practice of freewriting, my writing continued to get deeper. Soon I was writing with almost no interference from my busy, judgmental mind. Weird scenes, places I had never been, unbelievable characters, insights, dialogue—they all started pouring out of me during my freewriting sessions.

Instead of written prompts, I started using things like photographs, physical sensations, and scraps of remembered dreams to spark my freewriting sessions. Next I learned to create prompts that would lead my writing in a specific direction, and this made it possible to tackle larger projects on a bit-by-bit basis.

Eventually, I realized I contained within me a nonstop, powerful stream of creativity I could tap into *any time I wanted*. New ideas would appear *every time* I sat down and dropped into my freewriting practice. What did it mean?

It meant getting started with a writing project was the equivalent of finishing it. I knew how to sit down and write my way to the end of the piece I was working on, even though I knew a lot of my first drafts would be unusable.

As a writer facing constant deadlines, the craziness of these drafts was immaterial. Getting something down was the crux of the matter. From there, the drafts only required editing to turn them into finished copy.

This was incredibly liberating. But it also made me wonder about the true role of creativity, about how my internal wellspring connected to the larger world.

Creativity Is Everywhere

When I look around, it seems like creativity is everywhere. These days, people who do creative work get so much more respect than they did in the past, when only the most popular writers, artists, and musicians could attract large-scale attention.

Maybe people have learned to look at the world differently. Writers, inventors, Etsy craftspeople, indie musicians, YouTubers, street painters, mimes, choirs in shopping malls—creative energy is finding outlets everywhere.

Maybe this eruption of creativity comes from the democratization of the tools of creation. If all you need to make a movie is an iPhone, hundreds of millions of potential moviemakers are walking around at this moment.

In my parents' generation, loyalty and persistence were the most valued traits in society. If you did good work and watched out for the company (or the government or the bureaucracy), it would take care of you. It was an economic social contract.

The only problem with this arrangement was that as corporations got bigger, more efficient, and more globalized, jobs became increasingly specialized. In this kind of situation, it's more important for workers to accomplish their specialized tasks efficiently than for the "cogs in the machine" to think outside the box.

But who wants to spend forty years at the same job doing essentially the same thing? It doesn't suit the human drive for freedom.

No, we want more freedom, we want to do our thing, we want to live the life of the digital nomad, laptop in hand, traveling the world, making our living while doing what we love.

One of the most popular ways to get this freedom is by learning how to use the technology that enables us to do business online. "Guerrilla marketing" takes on a whole new meaning when a woman tapping at a computer in her home can gather a community of tens or hundreds of thousands of people, engage her audience, ignite a common passion in them, and compel them to act.

She might motivate them to act as voters, expressing their preferences. She might inspire them to attend a free educational event, participate in a special learning opportunity, or go on a trip to enhance their work, their lives, or their marriage. Or she might even create, almost from nothing, a *media channel* complete with an audience, themes, and regular programming, with the aim to teach, as well as to sell. This is just one of many, many models of sustainable businesses entrepreneurs build online, where a whole new model of cottage industries is spawning home-working millionaires with tremendous reach and clout.

Birth of a Book

These are some of the thoughts that occurred while I read my old blog post from 2010 on creativity. And reading it, I recognized that something had eluded me back then.

There was so much more to say on each of my bullet points, as well as more topics to write about. After all, creativity is at the heart of what I do, whether I'm writing, designing books, creating new products, or building and delivering presentations.

And that is how this book came to be. It is intended for writers and other creative types who need a boost or who have gotten trapped in a cul-de-sac in their work. It's not *intended* for groups to use in the pursuit of more creative action in their department or office (although it certainly could be used that way). It's meant to be more intimate than that because I hope to give you a new way of looking inside yourself to find some of the most common obstacles to creative work.

The only things I have to offer other people are the contents of my mind and heart and the accumulated experiences I've had over the years I've been involved in printing, design, advertising, direct mail, internet marketing, and book publishing. These experiences include the influence of lots of other people. I consider Jeff Walker to be one of my most important mentors in internet business, and he talks often about the power of the entrepreneur to change the world. In a very real way, authors who decide to publish their own books, like any other creative person who grabs hold of the tools of production and a means of distribution, are entrepreneurs, each running his or her own start-up operation.

Jeff claims entrepreneurs of all kinds are the real source of innovation and social progress, and they are the people who drive the most economic activity. This resonates with me because the changes we see are so often the result of one person's drive, ingenuity, and ambition to change the world. Hundreds or thousands of people may be required to put his or her ideas to practical use, but the impetus often starts with one person.

Creativity Now

This is why creativity is so important now. Nothing is more crucial than finding creative solutions to the problems we face, whether they are personal problems or difficulties in our community, in our nation, or on our planet. In addition, the world is constantly changing. Success in the future will rely on understanding how to creatively meet the challenge of constant change.

Making something new, something that never existed before, is the essence of creative action. That "something new" can be an extension of what came before, or it can break completely with everything we know.

Meeting the Muse

For the individual artist, creativity is paramount. If your life is driven, as mine has been, by the necessity to make something new, to make a difference, you know your ability to manifest your creativity in the world is an existential imperative. In other words, if you're someone who *has to* be creative, learning to access your creative source can mean the difference between life and death for a special, deep, and idiosyncratic part of you.

My job is to point out where the necessity to create meets obstacles, whether in the world or from our own unknown depths. My hope is that you, too, with the right help, can free your creative engine and harness it to create works you will leave for the world.

I want you to live, to write, to paint, to play your music, to sing at the sky, to dance when the spirit moves you. How? Attend to the quiet place inside where you'll find the torrent of images, ideas, words, sounds—a veritable maelstrom of invention—from which you can draw your own untarnished inventions that will make you who you are.

Go and create.

> The truth is, most of us discover where we are headed when we arrive.
>
> **—BILL WATTERSON**

1

You are absolutely unique, and what you have to offer the world cannot possibly be duplicated by anyone else.

Our individuality is the basis for all creativity. For some reason, you and I have a drive to create, to imagine new things, new worlds, new ideas and make them real. Unmistakably, this drive comes from somewhere inside us. But part of the problem we face is that our inner lives are largely unknowable, even to us.

Because of the way we're made, only a small bit of what we experience makes it into our active awareness. The rest—most of what we can sense about the world—gets submerged under the moment-to-moment demands of our lives.

We take in a huge amount that never gets into our conscious mind. Unrealized perceptions, intuitive connections, unspoken insights—these all become part of an unknown country, our own unconscious—the "dark side of the moon."

This is our curse—and our salvation, because in that underground world creativity runs strong, clear, and constant, even if it's largely unknown. It is ready to come to the surface to be a source of inspiration for your work, for yourself, for your mission here on Earth, if you're open to it.

We know each of us is unique. Our fingerprints are unique, and the irises of our eyes, too. But that's simply where our uniqueness starts. Every one of us has a different genetic inheritance from the complex mixing of the DNA of countless generations of ancestors (except those of you with an identical sibling).

Starting there, with our unique genetics, we each embark on our own journey through life, with families uniquely ours.

And don't forget, each of our parents is the result of a similarly complex process. And their parents before them. Think about how much complexity we have been imbued with due to the cascade of generations before us.

Meeting the Muse

So, rest assured, your mix of genetics and personal experience is completely unique to you. And when you add the element of time and realize we ourselves are subject to the laws of constant change, you can see how any moment you are experiencing is a moment only you can experience. In many ways, our art is simply the report we send back of how the world looks to us at any unique moment.

Treasure the uniqueness of now: it will never come again. Even if you try to recapture it, the light will be different, what you ate last night will be different, the scene will have changed, and, above all, *you will be different* because you have no choice but to keep changing.

Sink into this moment; it is where we truly come alive.

> The trick to creativity, if there is a single useful thing to say about it, is to identify your own peculiar talent and then to settle down to work with it for a good long time.
>
> **—STEPHEN JAY GOULD**

2

No one else can see what you see or has ever seen what you are seeing right now. Even the people sitting next to you are seeing something different from what you are seeing. This exact scene has never existed before and will never exist again.

Recognizing the "unique moment" is a seemingly simple step that can radically change your entire posture toward life. In reality, each moment is unique. We can tell because if we try to reproduce an event, a moment that evokes a vivid memory, we can't.

Meeting the Muse

Even if you put yourself back exactly in the same place at the same time of day, even if you ate the same lunch and wore the same clothes, *everything would be different*. The temperature would be different, both outside and within your body. You would be older. And, with about forty million cells dying every minute, *you* would be different, too, no matter how hard you try to stop yourself from changing.

This is not to say that many of the moments we pass through in our days aren't perfectly ordinary—they are. But even ordinary moments, if you look closely enough, are just as unique as those "special" ones.

When you realize this, you'll see that the combination of an utterly unique moment with the ordinary character of many of those same moments spurs creativity. As William Blake put it,

> To see a World in a Grain of Sand
> And a Heaven in a Wild Flower,
> Hold Infinity in the palm of your hand
> And Eternity in an hour.

The ordinary, in the right light, quickly becomes extraordinary if you choose to make it so.

Wherever you are reading this book right now, stop and look around. Maybe you've been in this same chair at Starbucks before, maybe you're lying on your bed, or perhaps you're sitting on the bus on your way to work.

Maybe you've seen the place you're in so often it has become invisible; when you look around, you see your past experiences here as much as you see the room itself. And that's okay because any moment works for this small experiment.

The secret is to stop. Look. Listen. Really tune in to where you are. Notice the air moving around you, sounds emerging in the distance, flickers of light, the angles made by shadows, faint aromas floating in the air, a video playing in another room, the pressure of an ill-fitting shoe—*everything*.

Life can seem like a nonstop film with intermissions for sleep, but when you break it down like this, it's more of a succession of moments. Stringing moments together allows a story to emerge, with meaning bound up in the action of each moment.

Learning to see the uniqueness of the moment allows you to fully occupy your life. Diving into this uniqueness gives you direct access to a rich vein of your own creative energy. The "eternal now," which awaits us in any moment that we remember to look for it, teems with energy—chaotic, expansive, destructive—and is filled with everything else that life contains.

Meeting the Muse

It is the only space into which the stream of creativity can emerge. To capture our creative output, we have to be in the moment with it. We'll talk more about this in the Exercise section later in this book. But right now, take a breath and give yourself a minute to treasure this moment: it will never come again.

> Exercising is a good analogy for writing. If you're not used to exercising, you want to avoid it forever. If you're used to it, it feels uncomfortable and strange not to. No matter where you are in your writing career, the same is true for writing. Even fifteen minutes a day will keep you in the habit.
>
> **—JENNIFER EGAN**

3

Other people may not understand what you're doing—which might be a good sign.

WHEN YOU'RE REALLY IN the creative flow, you can end up flowing right off the edge of what's known and accepted. Finding yourself "off the edge" can be a little disorienting. Why?

If there is nothing else like your idea, it might be hard to find a context that will help explain it. When folks have no context to help them, they might misunderstand or undervalue your creative efforts or the process you innovated. Although *you* see the way your work connects things that haven't been connected before, those connections can escape the notice of others.

Meeting the Muse

This is not necessarily a bad thing, but it's a lonely place to be.

Look, it may turn out your idea just doesn't work. It might be impractical, or it might not do what you initially thought it would. These things happen when ideas that were spun into existence in the free-wheeling expanse of our minds intersect with the real world. And that's perfectly normal; it happens all the time.

Creative people, no matter what field they are working in, are pioneers, trailblazers with no precursors. Until the world or your peers get to see and interact with your creation, you may well have to work in isolation.

John Updike, one of the most prominent writers of the twentieth century, was told early in his career that Random House would not publish his novel *Rabbit, Run* because it was "too divorced from reality."[1] Science fiction legend Ursula Le Guin was told that her novel *The Left Hand of Darkness* was "unreadable," yet it went on to win the 1969 Nebula Award for Best Novel and the 1970 Hugo Award, too.[2] Stories like these are numerous in every creative arena.

People who don't really get what you're trying to do may see your work as threatening to them in some way. A lot of people seem to be motivated by a drive for security, and new things, unpredictable processes, or surprising results may seem strange and unknowable to them and threatening to their world order.

Other creative people in your field may start to have questions themselves if you go off in a completely different and new direction. Some people will thank you for being a pioneer, but, unfortunately, many will respond with fear and ignorance.

Be clear what it is you are looking for from other people. Do you want encouragement? Understanding? Collaboration? Or just a big round of applause?

As a creative, you can choose whom to share your work with and whom to avoid. Experience will guide you when it comes to friends and family, but you may need to be more careful when you're considering sharing your work with other creatives, vendors, supporters, or fans.

Oh, you thought it was going to be all flowers and rainbows? Sorry to disappoint you, but all of this is just another way to say that whatever happens, stay true to your vision. If one project ends up not working out, you'll still learn a lot in the process, and as long as you're learning, there is hope.

> Creativity is piercing the mundane to find the marvelous.
>
> **—BILL MOYERS**

4

Avoid taking credit for your good ideas; then you won't have to accept blame for the ones that don't work out.

Okay, let's be honest. I'll go first.

I have no idea where my own thoughts come from—I mean any of them. Sure, some are predictable, simply because some thoughts have been closely associated with other thoughts for a long time. Other thoughts are a repetition of earlier thoughts that have become connected in our minds. Like, if I say "Marco," what do you hear in your head? I hear an answering "Polo."

But that's not my point.

If you could watch the surface of your mind—where thoughts appear—and you managed to catch your own thoughts as they arise, you might be reminded of a glass of champagne. In a tall, thin champagne glass, you can see bubbles form and then release, floating up to the surface of the liquid, where, with a pop, they emit their tiny-bubble content of air, creating effervescence.

So, too, in the champagne glass of my mind, if I watch in just the right way, I can see thoughts popping into view, little bursts of recognition or anxiety or joy or irritation or criticism or nonsense or nothing. Each one persists for a moment before it's crowded out as another thought appears.

When you're in a creative process, you enter a flow. Ideas seem to travel directly from your brain to your fingers flying over the keyboard (or whatever it is you do), appearing on a sheet of paper or a screen in front of you. In this process, you might reasonably start to think you are mostly an engaged spectator to the tumble of words or music or ideas unfolding in your mind.

The great thing about this is that this posture toward our own creative thoughts lifts the weight of credit and blame from us.

Credit and blame reside on the opposite sides of the same coin. To believe in one is to believe in both—in a whole "judicial" system that dispenses credit and blame according to some measure that is never clearly defined but each of us thinks we know.

We judge some of our thoughts to be better than others, and by that I mean they are more innovative, more connecting, or more empathetic, piercing deeper into our subject. When a thought like this arises, it's very exciting. It opens new vistas and makes connections we didn't even realize were there.

But we can't really take credit for these thoughts, can we?

The same is true of the thoughts on the other side of the coin. You know the ones: the cruel thoughts, nasty judgments, regrets, or should-have-beens—the tsunami of criticism about ourselves and others.

When we try to ignore the dark side of our nature, we just give it more power. To harness our interior resources, we need to first acknowledge that they exist.

Years ago, when I was going through a tough transition in my life, I had recurring visions of machine-gunning the person I held responsible for the pain I was suffering. This image was incredibly vivid and visceral. I could feel the buck of the gun and smell the gunpowder as bullets riddled his big, fat body. The vision alone excited me in a disturbing yet satisfying way.

But lots of other thoughts visit us in the night, from the monsters that seemed to lurk under our beds when we were kids to the images that leap to mind when a sound wakes us up at night. And I haven't even mentioned the bizarre and fantastical apparitions and fantasies that boil their way to the surface when we dream.

Certainly, we're responsible for how we *act* on the thoughts we have. That's where we define our humanity. But that's it. If you want to be able to drop the self-judgment that cripples so many creative people, you may also have to give up taking credit—even when things go exactly as you intended.

Treasure your creativity; it is an unparalleled gift. Just don't imagine yourself the ultimate author. Craft and artistry help us make something that will inspire others, but the original creative impulses arise from the unknown within each of us.

> This is what we—as artists—have always done. We take our pain and we transform it into some kind of narrative, some show or story, something . . . else. We frame our trauma as best we can, and we offer it up.
>
> **—AMANDA PALMER**

5

My father told me, "Never be the only one in a room doing something." He was right—but not always.

STAYING TUNED IN TO what your colleagues and peers are doing can be stimulating to your own work. On the other hand, the creative impulse sometimes demands we break from the past and move in a new, bold, different direction. When everyone is zigging, you can stand out by being the person with zag.

Still, sometimes it's best to find your place within the range of your community.

Let me tell you a story about a wedding I went to at San Francisco's Union Club, a very posh location at the top of Nob Hill. No one had spelled out the dress code for the event in advance, so my wife, Jill, and I dressed as we normally would for a formal wedding. We walked up the wide sandstone steps to the club expecting a good time.

How surprised do you think I was when I stopped at the entrance, looked out onto 150 or 200 guests, and saw every single man in the room was dressed in a tuxedo? I was wearing a lovely light gray English suit.

For the rest of the evening, I could not have felt more out of place than if I had walked in naked with a pineapple on my head.

Eventually, I ran into a couple of other men who had "missed the memo" about the dress code, and we commiserated, huddling in shared shame and isolation. I'm sure it's the kind of experience my father was trying to protect me from when he cautioned me not to be the only one doing something—that's what fathers do.

But consider this. If you are marketing, being different is exactly what you want. After all, I was the easiest person to find in the whole venue. Everyone else, lost in a sea of men dressed like penguins, was anonymous.

If this had been a situation in which I wanted to market or create something, I would have been very happy. Sadly, it wasn't, and my time at the wedding wasn't much fun.

Meeting the Muse

You, on the other hand, need to know for yourself if you're standing out because you blew it or if your isolation is a sign of creative originality and soon people will realize it and *come to you*.

Being a creative artist isn't always easy, and sometimes you are going to feel like the guy in a gray suit in a roomful of tuxedos—or worse. You might start to think something is different about you, and there may be an element of truth in that because, by their nature, art and creativity are wholly involved with the new, with things that have never been seen before, with original creations bursting into existence.

My advice? Breathe deeply, and learn to live with it. After all, do you have an alternative?

In many creative fields, the true genius of creativity or innovation may not be recognized until long after the creators are gone. This includes creative artists who, while they lived, may have made other people's lives more challenging. The painter Vincent Van Gogh, for example, was at best a difficult companion. He once went after a colleague with a razor, and he sold only one painting during his lifetime. He survived on the generosity of his brother Théo. Stories like this are common among creative types, so let's all get used to being the "odd fish."

Be grateful for the gift you've been given.

> In times of strife, we have our imagination, we have our creative impulse, which are things that are more important than material things. They are the things that we should magnify.
>
> **—PATTI SMITH**

6

Let what you've created speak for itself.

IN OUR FREEWRITING SESSIONS our teacher, Suzanne, would often remind us to avoid on-ramping and off-ramping. At first, I had no idea what she meant.

While freewriting, we don't judge what we're writing; we give ourselves permission to write whatever wants to be written. This is the biggest challenge: learning how to get out of our own way to allow whatever arises to express itself without any filtering on our part.

Our creative work doesn't need any qualifiers, preambles, explanations, hedges, and disclaimers when we share it with the world:

- "I haven't had time to do any editing on this story . . ."
- "Let me explain to you the events leading up to this piece . . ."
- "The context for this article was critical in deciding to write it because . . ."

Creatives naturally hesitate when introducing their work to other people or to the world at large. After all, they have a lot to be concerned about.

What if people misunderstand what you've said? Maybe they won't get the all-important context this piece occupies in relation to your other works, how you were feeling that day, what you were trying to say that you're not sure really got said?

Don't you want people to be able to fully appreciate the work?

Unfortunately, this kind of uncertainty leads to what Suzanne called on-ramping—attempts to prepare the way, put the work in context, or explain what it is beforehand. None of this is going to help, and you probably already knew it, and that's one reason you were nervous to begin with.

The explanations are all apologies of one sort or another offered by an insecure part of you that seems to think you should apologize for the very act of creating.

Meeting the Muse

You stepped outside the "acceptable" zone, dared to expose a part of yourself, and made a statement. So why fling your insecurities in the face of an expectant listener? Let the work speak for itself.

First, your work deserves its chance at life. It arose, unbidden, from your creative depths. Then you worked on it, polished it, perfected your story, painting, play, innovation, whatever it is.

Explanations can come later, but at the precious moment when you open your hands and let your work fly free, don't offer a long on-ramp of disclaimers and conditions.

And don't do it after your audience has just seen or read or listened to or looked at your work, either. Save it for another time. That's off-ramping, saving up all your explanations while patiently waiting for people to absorb what you've just offered. You feel like you're lying in wait for your prey and then pouncing on them to extract their real feelings about what you've done.

With a small amount of self-discipline, it doesn't have to be that way.

What will help? Learn to bear the silence around your work. That silence is part of the effect your work is having, and it can be treasured as an integral part of the work itself.

Joel Friedlander

Now when I'm asked to share my work, I take a deep breath and stay quiet as I wait for explanations buzzing in my head to quiet down. This pause creates just the right space in the world into which I can offer my work.

If I'm reading to others, the pause creates a silence, without embellishment; then I can start to read. If I'm showing something visual, such as a design, the space created is just as effective.

You'll never find out the true effect your work has if you're constantly on-ramping and off-ramping. So let your work speak for itself.

All creative work builds on what came before. So run toward influence instead of away from it. Read tons of books, go to museums, concerts and movies, take long walks, etc. Be always on the lookout for inspiration and carry a notebook with you wherever you go so you never lose an idea.

—AUSTIN KLEON

7

Believe in your work, champion it bravely, and support it with passion. If you don't, why should anyone else believe in it?

When you're creating something that has never existed before, advocating passionately for your work and your vision is imperative.

New things can be novel, attractive, intriguing. But they can also threaten a world that's built on old ideas. Colleagues who are using an old way of doing things may not take kindly to your innovation. Friends may not understand your new creation. Reviewers and critics may have no idea what to make of it. But as we know, your creation contains a piece of you, ineffable though it may be.

Here is an example. My friend, the late photographer Tom Millea, almost singlehandedly brought the "lost" art of printing with platinum and palladium back into use in the United States. Through long years of experimenting and showing the ethereal, subtle prints he was making, he stuck to his vision even when others thought he was wasting his time.

After all, his beautiful prints weren't black and white, like most "serious" photographic works at the time. But they had a delicate quality and a tonal range that silver prints could never equal.

Eventually, his work paid off, and now fine art photographic prints made this way command some of the highest prices in the market.

So don't be hesitant, fearful, or ashamed of what you've produced. Be proud. Stand tall as you present your poetry, your new theory, your book to the world. Let yourself glow with the satisfaction you rightly feel at giving birth to something entirely new.

This doesn't mean that every single idea you have is fabulous and will change the world—far from it. All creative people know that they will experience many false starts, failures of understanding, unexpected obstacles, and other circumstances they hadn't anticipated. Many ideas will fall by the wayside, even though they were intoxicating when they first arose.

It's up to you to know when your idea is ready to meet the world. And when it is, you must get entirely behind it. This will help orient you toward success and rev your engine to market or promote your work in the world.

The more you champion yourself and your work, the more likely you are to attract others who feel the same way about it. They will, given time, become passionate advocates who help you make your way as you continue on your creative journey.

> To know what you're going to draw, you have to begin drawing.
>
> **—PABLO PICASSO**

8

Put yourself into everything you produce.

When I was young and learning how to write and make my way in the world, I worked at many factory jobs to keep food on the table. I always learned something in these jobs and often saw great camaraderie among the workers on the factory floor.

Despite the learning and camaraderie, I worked at these jobs for the absolute minimum amount of time necessary to collect enough money to buy food and pay the rent for a few months. Then I would quit.

What drove me away from factory work? Why did I want to get out as soon as I could? Because the work I did there was completely impersonal. As a young man I

Meeting the Muse

was willing to trade a few months of tedium and dehumanization for a stretch of complete freedom. But soon enough, I would be back looking at the job listings.

I spent a few years living this way, working in cardboard box fabrication, plastic coffee can lid manufacturing, bank safety device assembly, and various other hire-me-today type of jobs. But I recognized an inescapable truth: for the factory owner, many workers are not much more than replaceable parts in the manufacturing process.

For example, one summer I had a job at a sheet metal fabricating plant making items such as hot air ducts. One task required me to sit in front of a press brake, a hulking machine with huge jaws that held a set of molds.

A wooden pallet loaded with hundreds of sheets of galvanized steel sat on one side of me; an empty pallet waited on the other side. I picked up one sheet of steel, positioned it between the molds, and then pulled both hands back. To activate the machine, I had to simultaneously press two switches located about three feet apart, which ensured that my hands were away from the moving parts of the machine.

When both switches were tripped, the molds slowly smashed together, bending the steel into the shape of the molds. When the machine yawned open, I removed the now-bent piece of steel and stacked it on the pallet. When one pallet was finished, a worker on a forklift would take it away and drop another in its place.

So the process was pick up the steel, align it properly in the machine, trip the switches to activate the machine, take the bent steel out, and stack it. I did this over and over again, one sheet at a time.

Can you feel the soul-deadening repetition in this story? Part of the oppressive feeling comes from the entirely impersonal nature of the work. I could have been replaced by anyone capable of moving both hands at the same time. That's not a very high bar, is it?

But deeper than the impersonal work was the product I was producing, the outcome of my efforts. Looking at the stacks of nicely bent steel, I could not see my own influence on the process anywhere. These air ducts would look exactly the same no matter who made them because they were really the work of the people who designed the machines and the molds that were used to create them—not me, who only shuffled pieces back and forth.

This is the exact opposite of creative work, and it's the reason that I had to leave each of these jobs—and I had many of them—as soon as I could.

Meeting the Muse

In the years since then, I've been better able to integrate the various sides of my life, and I fully understand from my own experience that we have many identities, sometimes contradictory ones, within us. But when I was young, like a lot of other young people, I felt that I had to choose who I was going to be and stick with it. Life was all rather black and white—and confusing, too.

Keep in mind I came of age in the 1960s: I marched on the Pentagon in 1967, went to love-ins, and did all the rest of the things we "hippies" were doing back then. So the choice was to become part of some huge machine in which individuals were prized mostly for their ability to contribute to the corporation's bottom line or try to live inside my own humanity, dedicating myself to principles that seemed to be a lot deeper and more important than net profits.

These days life seems a lot more nuanced, more specific, and less abstract for me. Looking at the work people do today, it seems any task you're engaged in that isn't entirely mechanized will somehow allow you to embody something of yourself in the work.

For instance, if you and I were in the same kitchen and had the exact same ingredients and tools and we each produced a cheese omelet, those omelets would be different, wouldn't they? So it's not really the ingredients or the tools that imbue a final product with its essence. When those ingredients are combined with all the accumulated knowledge, skill, and experience of the maker, the result is uniquely the product of its creator.

It doesn't matter whether you're writing a blog post, painting a landscape, innovating an industrial process, or creating anything that arises from your inner processes. Everything you create carries a bit of yourself in it. We are used to thinking this way about artisanal products, which often carry the story of their creation as part of their appeal. Or they are branded with their founder's name.

But what about the way you realized you could achieve much higher productivity at some of your frequent tasks by rearranging the order in which you did them? Isn't that creative? Or maybe you took a walk and you realized how nature blends colors in a constantly shifting seasonal palette, and then you incorporated that insight into your own decorating or into products you create for a specific market.

In every creative endeavor, we leave a trace of ourselves, no matter how small or quiet it may seem to others. This gives us a kind of ownership over the products of our creative endeavors, an ownership that never fades away.

Meeting the Muse

The way we intuit something about an artist from her painting and sense the invisible essence she put into it—even several hundred years later—is a kind of proof she is still in there today.

Don't you love being a creative?

> Passion is one great force that unleashes creativity, because if you're passionate about something, then you're more willing to take risks.
>
> **—YO-YO MA**

9

Learn when to share an idea with a friend and when to guard it as the most precious secret.

HAVING A NEW IDEA can be exciting—so exciting you want to rush out and share it with friends, with strangers, with anyone who will listen! After all, you may get a great reaction, a confidence booster, and lots of encouragement to continue developing the idea, and that would make you feel great about what you're doing.

Should you share this new idea?

Maybe the reaction is not going to be what you expected. The person you share your idea with may not react very favorably, and if your idea is still loose and amorphous, if it hasn't really taken shape, you stand the

Meeting the Muse

risk of losing the energy the idea was carrying when it first popped into your mind.

In the face of criticism, you may not be able to stop yourself from thinking, "Maybe the person is right. How could I have thought this idea was so good?"

It might be better instead to step back and realize that maybe the person you asked was not the right person to listen to your idea. Maybe he's too close to you and cannot be objective. What if the person you're sharing with has a headache or got yelled at by her boss at work today or is worrying about a sick child?

You can't allow your confidence to be shattered so easily. After you hear negative comments, your idea may look quite different to you. And while we all need to remain open to the feedback we get from people who are constructive, if your idea is still in a conceptual phase, now may not be the best time to share it.

All those who create must learn this lesson for themselves. In the early stages of a project, you probably want to talk about it. You may be tempted to elaborate on your idea, explaining why it's a necessary part of your creative process. Make sure *you* are ready for your idea to see the light of day. Be cautious. Once it is spoken, you cannot easily get back what you've said.

Here's an example. Years ago, I was working on a book that was important to me for personal reasons. As I was writing I was sharing it with a friend, who gave me a lot of positive feedback, encouraging me to continue writing. It felt like the wind in my sails.

One day a new character popped up unexpectedly and gave a whole new dimension to the story. When this new character arrived, my friend had a negative reaction so strong she didn't want to read the story any longer. Her criticism was delivered with a lot of force.

Afterward, I realized my feelings about the character—and the book—were changing. If I had remained true to my own creative vision, I would have continued writing, but the confusion my friend's criticism produced persuaded me to put the whole project aside for a while. You may have already guessed the end of this story: I never picked up the book again.

The lesson I learned from this is there is a time for your friends and colleagues to help you bring your book into reality, and it will come later in the creative process.

For now, mum's the word. Learn to discriminate which friends are a better resource for you while your idea is in its infancy. Or control your need to share until the project can stand on its own merits.

Meeting the Muse

> The free, exploring mind of the individual human is the most valuable thing in the world.
>
> **—JOHN STEINBECK**

10

*Don't let **perfect** become the enemy of **good**. Being productive in the world will require compromise somewhere along the way.*

WRITERS ARE ARTISANS, IN a way. Wordsmiths, like many other kinds of artisans, ply their trade alone, so it's easy for them to fall into what I think of as the "artisan's curse."

It starts with the quest for perfection. This could be the search for the perfect scene, the best word choice, or endless color balancing in search of some ideal tonal vibration.

Every art has techniques to master, and when we're learning a technique, we compare our work to an ideal of some kind to judge our progress. That's all well and good, but it can leave us with the feeling that our work must be just as good as the model before it's ready to be released into the world.

It's difficult to criticize an artisan for wanting to make his work perfect. After all, an artisan's work will represent him in the world, so why *shouldn't* he take as much time and effort as needed to bring his work as close as possible to the ideal? This attitude can be a problem if he wants to make a real-world impact.

Too often I've found myself at the computer endlessly tweaking layouts, experimenting with a few more typefaces, and adjusting spacing, with all the elements of a design in a constant evolution of *becoming*, never quite *being* a final product. I'm sitting in the back of the cave, "polishing my stone," content to continually disassemble and reassemble the pieces of whatever I'm working on, looking endlessly for ways to improve it.

Of course, if you keep doing this, your work will never make it into the marketplace. It will stay in a state of getting incrementally better, and the changes you make will have an ever-decreasing benefit.

In other words, nothing will "ship." No matter how perfect I tried to make my creation, my efforts had no effect whatsoever because during that time, no one else saw my work.

Creativity without producing something isn't very fulfilling.

Take a step back. How much of your original intention does your work accomplish right now? Are you on the wrong end of the 80/20 principle? Also known as the Pareto principle, it recommends spending 80 percent of our time on the 20 percent of our work that creates the most impact.

Keep your original goal in mind. I'm guessing the goal isn't to make something that's perfect and fully articulated in every possible way. Something more visceral is probably behind it, something affecting you much more directly, something you can get only from launching your project, releasing it to find its way in the world, pushing it out of the nest.

Is it perfect? Maybe not. Does it accomplish *most* of what you wanted to accomplish when you started? Could you launch it now and come back with a "second edition" further down the line?

If so, ship it out the door.

As creatives, we can use our imaginative and artistic abilities to conjure works of one kind or another, seemingly from nothing. When we learn how to send these works into the cultural marketplace, we gain the ability to build a powerful and productive career.

So don't let all the good that can come from your efforts disappear in a misguided search for something "perfect."

> The creative person is ... shuffling his information at all times, even when he is not conscious of it. The presence of others can only inhibit this process, since creation is embarrassing. For every new good idea you have, there are a hundred, ten thousand foolish ones, which you naturally do not care to display.
>
> **—ISAAC ASIMOV**

11

Doing something worthwhile takes time—and training, preparation, and resolve. You'll need to have some skills to overcome your own resistance.

SURE, BEING CREATIVE CAN be exciting, it can make us feel more alive, and it can connect us to resources we may have overlooked. But let's not kid ourselves. Many artists claim their work is "1 percent inspiration, 99 percent perspiration."

Ironically, the biggest reason sticking to a goal is so hard comes from *within us*. I'm talking about resistance from your unconscious mind. Why does this happen?

Just setting a goal can evoke a force from within that is opposed to any forward movement. It's the

Meeting the Muse

psychological reflection of Isaac Newton's third law of physics: for every action, there is an equal and opposite reaction. When you push harder against this resistance, it stiffens in response.

Whole books have been written about this resistance, and it's crucial to remember that before you set your goal, there was no resistance. In a way, we create the resistance simply by wanting to accomplish something specific. Diabolical, isn't it?

What kind of resistance am I talking about? It's the resistance you encounter when you realize the difficulty of going beyond the first couple of paragraphs or the first few pages once your original inspiration has played itself out and you wonder, Where do I go from here? Or it could be the thoughts that pop into your mind, insinuating that maybe you were completely wrong about this writing (painting/photography/design) thing; it really isn't for you at all. Or perhaps, no matter how much you try to carve out time to work on your project, there always seems to be a sick child, a crisis at work, or tickets bought months in advance.

And so it goes. The world is a place that's often beautiful, but it seems to have no particular interest in helping us reach our goals. Sometimes it feels like we have to do everything on our own.

For example, I once spent four months putting together a training course for authors, fighting through the resistance when I could. But the closer I came to the end of the project, the slower everything seemed to go. Even during the very last week, as I worked crazy hours to try to keep the project on track, it took everything I had to just keep going: one more PDF, one more transcript. On and on it went, seemingly without end.

When you're captured by the resistance, almost anything looks more enjoyable than what you've assigned yourself to do. Maybe today suddenly seems to be the perfect day to clean up the garage or to do the bookkeeping that's fallen behind. Why struggle with editing your second draft? It's a good day to paint the spare bedroom.

Many people have come up with ways to overcome this resistance, but for me it has been important to see it at work, to watch, sometimes with alarm, as my precious goals are defeated by inaction, inattention, or neglect. This is the trail that resistance leaves.

These are some of the ways I've found to make progress despite resistance:

- Attaching something pleasurable to the task at hand, for instance, doing a tiresome editing task while sitting outside in a beautiful environment.

Meeting the Muse

- Keeping focused on a goal to win a reward, like promising myself a chocolate cookie at a predetermined milestone in the work.
- Best of all, establishing a habit to simply show up and work. Nothing is more powerful in my own work than the habits I've established. So, if I do most of my writing in the mornings, I will sit down and work at the appointed time because it's become a habit to do so.

Big projects especially will take determination to complete. But don't worry, your determination will bloom with regular use. Your persistence and ability to see and deal with your own resistance will grow like a muscle until you are truly a brawny creative, able to leap tall projects at a single bound.

As painter Chuck Close says, "Inspiration is for amateurs; the rest of us just show up and get to work."

So just stay with it.

> Inventing something cool that can't be implemented isn't creative. It's mostly a waste.
>
> **—SETH GODIN**

12

Say yes to your own creative time.

We mature when we learn to discipline ourselves, when we're able to measure long-term gains against near-term satisfaction; it's something we all go through. But somewhere along the way we can lose the easy *yes* that was so natural when we were young.

Let's recover our ability to say yes with enthusiasm and passion.

Say yes to yourself by establishing a boundary around your chosen creative time. I know busy people think there isn't any more time in the day to add creative work. But saying "There isn't time!" doesn't help.

I struggled with this problem for many years—too many, to be honest. None of us want to think about all the things we could have done if we had only made different decisions long ago.

I don't like to think of all the writing I could have been doing during those years, either. But I was stuck between the desire to express myself creatively and the hard fact of working for a living at a job that seemed to leave little time for anything else.

I was jealous of people who could spend their mornings writing. My friend Karl found a working solution to the problem. Most mornings, Karl would get up early to go for a run. When he decided to write a book, he continued getting up early and preparing as if he was going to go running. He would put on his running clothes and running shoes, just like always. But instead of running, he sat at his keyboard and worked on his book for the same amount of time he would have been running. After about a year, the book was done.

For me, the breakthrough came when I began to enforce priorities in my day. Here's an example. What if your doctor suggested that you start an exercise routine that takes an hour a day? And what if she told you that without this specific exercise, your health would deteriorate to the point that life would become a whole lot less enjoyable? How hard would you work to make sure you found that hour?

When something—like your health—is a high priority you *make* time for it, don't you? You have no choice, so you rearrange your responsibilities and call on friends and relatives for help, whatever you must do to accommodate your need.

My main creative work is writing. After many frustrating years bemoaning my lack of time, this breakthrough made it obvious what I needed to do.

I created a two-pronged strategy. First, I set aside time in the morning to do my creative work. I blocked it out on my calendar, and when I had to arrange meetings or other appointments, that time was simply unavailable, so those things got scheduled at other times.

Did I miss those hours taken out of my schedule for creative work? Not really. Over the years, I've frequently verified Parkinson's law: work expands to fill the time allotted to its completion. For example, if my editor needs my article by Friday at noon, I'll be polishing it Friday morning. But if he needs it on Wednesday, no matter what day I get started, I'll be proofreading it Wednesday morning.

Because of Parkinson's law, allotting fewer hours to my workday had virtually no effect; everything got done anyway. If you think this won't work for you, see tips in

"Establish a Daily Creative Practice" in the exercise section of this book.

Second, I used that time to get out of my office. I don't know about you, but when I'm sitting at my desk, creative work is interrupted by the constant stream of alerts, updates, mail, messages, pings, notices, and all the other attention grabbers that flash across our screens and populate our days.

I began to write in my car, which wasn't too bad. With a cup of coffee, a fully charged iPad, and a wireless keyboard, I could park wherever I liked and have a quiet place to write for an hour.

Eventually, I relocated to a nearby coffee shop, which has turned out to be a great environment for me. There's just enough distraction, forcing me to focus on the work at hand, yet not so much that I'm drawn away from what I'm focusing on.

Over the last several years, I've established a routine. Every day I can, I go to the coffee shop, drink big cups of green tea, and pound away on my laptop. Whether I'm working on a book project, blog posts, articles for publication, or more fanciful work, this routine has been an incredible boon.

Little by little, an hour at a time, I've been able to turn out tons of work. When I get up to leave the coffee shop, heading back to the office to confront my overflowing in-box, I have a palpable satisfaction and the impetus to keep going tomorrow with my incremental progress.

You can do this, too. It may require some adjustments, but once you make that commitment to yourself, you will find ways to keep it.

Consider your creative time sacred; hold on to it with all your might. It's your ticket to the world of living the creative life. And like the doctor who advises her patient to do a specific exercise every day for physical health, I'm prescribing this daily creative work for your emotional and spiritual health. Because if you really want to create, and you don't allow yourself the time to do it, you will suffer the consequences in unhappiness, frustration, and eventually, regret.

Don't let that happen to you. Build strong fences around your creative time; then relax into it and get to work. You'll be so glad you did.

The worst enemy to creativity is self-doubt.

—SYLVIA PLATH

13

Be present during the process of creation. If you are, the letdown or anticlimax of completion will never happen.

Being present to what's happening to us in real time—as it is occurring—is a skill people spend a lifetime learning, so I don't want to give the impression that you can just flip a switch inside yourself and turn on the presence. (See chapter 27 for more on this topic.) Still, it's crucial to learn this skill to fully live your life, especially if you hope to unbind your creative impulses.

In a simple way, saying we have the ability to be present in our own moment-by-moment experiences implies we can also be absent from our lives. That seems odd to a lot of people. After all, you are here, how could you be absent?

Yet this is an actual phenomenon—not a metaphor. So how can you know when you're present and when you've been absent? Think about things that happen to all of us at one time or another:

- You realize you haven't heard the last few minutes of conversation with the person sitting across from you because you've been thinking about something she said earlier in the conversation.
- You hear yourself saying the exact words you promised repeatedly you'd never say again.
- You notice you've just driven past the highway exit you were supposed to take.
- You identify the bad odor wafting through the house as the smell of your kettle burning dry.

I could go on, but I'm sure you've got the idea.

Being absent can be very productive for creatives because it's likely we've gone into a psychic zone our teachers might have called "daydreaming" back in our school days. At least that's what my teachers were always writing on my report cards: "Joel is intelligent and seems to understand the lessons, but very often I see he isn't paying attention and seems to be staring out the window."

Meeting the Muse

But what I was staring at wasn't the scene outside the windows—I was staring into my own imagination. Weren't you doing that, too?

So let's just say there are, for the sake of convenience, two different ways we can be "awake." (Of course, this is a ridiculous idea because all of us who pay even the slightest attention to our own fluctuating inner states will know immediately our awareness slides along a scale of vastly different states of attention.) Let's call the first way "absence" and the second "presence."

All those examples I listed in my bullet list are ways in which absence occurs in our day-to-day lives. Conversely, when we are keenly aware of where we are; what's happening around us; the smells, textures, shifting light and shadow; the sounds of the environment; the emotional tone inside us; and the energetic connection we have with others nearby, those are times when we are fully present in our own lives.

Memories, too, are influenced by these different mental states. When we are forced into the present because of a shock of some kind, the memory created is indelible, permanent. Memories of times when we were more or less absent quickly fade away.

For instance, when I was living in California in the 1970s, I got to experience an earthquake for the first time in my life. In the small hours of the morning, the quake jolted me awake. I can still remember the incredible feeling of the building moving beneath me as the furniture swayed and small objects banged onto the floor.

The next earthquake I experienced happened as I walked into a large printing plant near Sacramento. As soon as the earthquake started, all the workers froze where they were standing and stopped what they were doing. The lights flashed as the fixtures swayed from the ceiling. In my memory, it's like it happened yesterday.

When another earthquake struck, I was grilling on the back patio of our house as my son came out the kitchen door to join me. We stopped as the ground itself seemed to be deciding whether to stay the solid base that we were used to or to turn into a viscous liquid right beneath our feet. We just stood, looking at each other in silence, waiting for the shaking to stop.

I can remember each of these moments with total clarity. The events cut through whatever was happening at the moment with a much more urgent reality, thrusting me into real presence.

Compare this to whatever you were doing yesterday. Was there a moment with as much power—so much

Meeting the Muse

that you can be sure you'll remember it ten or twenty years from now?

Although earthquakes can create moments that are both indelible and instructive, waiting for one isn't a very good strategy to be more present in your life. But "Pay Attention" in the exercise section is a great place to start.

Learning to increase the presence in our lives at the moments when it really matters can have a profound effect on our creative process. Bringing a fully engaged awareness into your everyday activities can literally change your life.

Opportunities to increase presence, surprisingly, are all around us, and some of the best reside in normal day-to-day activities. Washing dishes, folding laundry, raking leaves, and many other semiautomatic tasks take only a small amount of attention. This leaves the mind free—if you can separate from your own thoughts—to notice new things, to be anchored in the observation of the world around you.

Every human seems to have the ability to create this presence. It requires nothing but your attention, yet we spend vast stretches of our lives pretty much asleep to most of what's going on around us and inside us.

Being more present can connect you to your own deep springs of creativity. Give it a try.

> Just set one day's work in front of the last day's work. That's the way it comes out. And that's the only way it does.
>
> **—JOHN STEINBECK**

14

Creativity can involve action—or not.

OVER THE COURSE OF my life, creative work has seemed to occupy two different and almost opposite poles of activity.

At one pole, I might be daydreaming, noodling while in the shower or washing the dishes, or mindlessly watching the landscape roll by while navigating down the highway. Although events are happening around me, they have been pushed into the background or deep into the unconscious, only occasionally tossing up scraps of ideas or half-formed thoughts.

It's a trancelike state in some ways, but many people find moments like these to be some of the most productive in their creative lives.

At the other pole, I'm actively in the process of creation. Whether it's writing an article, working through options on a book design, or tinkering with a new recipe, I'm actively engaged.

You could look at it this way: most creative ideas seem to occur when you contemplate, daydream, think long thoughts, or "sleep on it," but bringing these ideas to life—laying down paint, crafting sentences, working through the details—is also part of your creativity. In fact, the ideas that originally inspired you will likely be changed, adapted, and modified once you begin implementing them in the real world.

These two poles are completely different types of activities, and both will likely come into play in your creative endeavors. Usually, you start with an idea, a spark that wakes you up to a new possibility. In some cases, it's a bolt of electricity running through you.

But what happens next? Do you run off immediately to make something of your new idea? Maybe you need time to fully appreciate its implications, in which case you might profit from giving yourself plenty of idle time to let the thought take shape, show its different sides, and connect to other ideas.

Something else well known to creative people is that while you're busy painting or sawing or banging on your

Meeting the Muse

keyboard, everyone can see you're at work. But at the other pole, the work isn't obvious. You might even be criticized for "just sitting around," "daydreaming," or "spacing out."

"Stop staring out the window and get to work!" How many times have I heard that sentence, even in my own mind? Too many times.

What to do? Maybe the best approach is grant yourself the space your process needs, whatever it may be. Others may not understand how your creative mind works, but you know the quiet time is just as important as the active time.

So, take your time. Ideas can be improved by a slow mental roasting, like a chicken self-basting on a rotisserie. Turning ideas slowly in your mind gives them the opportunity to expand, connect, and become ripe for action. This time allows you to wait until you are ready to act, to move to the other pole.

Respect the process. The quiet times are just as critical to creative output as the more active times. And if people ask why you appear to not be doing anything, just tell them that's exactly what you are doing: nothing.

> [Creativity is] taking what's in front of you and everybody else and making something new out of it.
>
> **—AUSTIN KLEON**

15

Tools have never created anything. People create with the tools that are available.

Are you a writer? Technology has had a huge impact on the way we write, starting with advancements in papermaking and taking off with the late-nineteenth-century invention of the typewriter, which tied writers to the machines on which they wrote.

This development—the marriage of writer and machine—has influenced almost all writers ever since. The tools we use for writing and editing continue to go through radical changes as new paradigms and metaphors inform the electronic tools we now use for our work.

I've been around for a while and have had a chance to observe this evolution over the last fifty years, as digitization has rolled over the original "typing machine" and created an entirely new world of tools for the writer's trade.

My first book was written—and rewritten—on an Olivetti Lettera, a portable manual typewriter that functioned as the "laptop" of its day. It came with a carry case and was light and easy to take with you no matter where you wanted to do your writing. Its minty green metal exterior was far friendlier than the hulking black typewriters of the era, too.

Using a manual typewriter turns writing into a physical workout, one that reflects your mood while you're writing. Are you stroking the keys as you flow through the process of transferring mental images into words made of letters? Or are you bashing your keyboard, your letters making deep impressions as the metal keys strike the paper?

A few years ago, I wandered down to our local Apple store and found among the young people in their blue shirts an older woman who, I felt, might be able to answer a question.

"There's something the matter with your new Apple keyboards," I told her. "Since I've been using these

Meeting the Muse

low-profile keyboards, my fingers hurt, especially on the tips where I hit the letters. Do you have anything better?"

She looked at me coolly. "Can I ask if you learned to type on a manual typewriter?" she asked.

"Yes, it was years ago. Why do you ask?"

"Because you need to *unlearn* what you learned back then. These keyboards are meant to be *tapped*, not hit. Try touching them lightly; you'll find it makes a world of difference," she said. "And no, we don't have any other keyboards."

Of course, she was perfectly right. I was pounding my flat keyboard, and that's why my fingers hurt.

I don't recommend manual typewriters for today's authors since the tools of writing have gone through at least three generations of evolution: the invention of the electric typewriter; the move to digitization through big-computer-based word-processing workstations, and the devolution of those same tools to individuals through personal computers.

Believe me, editing a book written on a manual typewriter is no picnic. If you do it, you will soon learn where the metaphor of "cut and paste" originated—with a big pair of scissors and a jar of rubber cement. When working on my first book, I would cut the manuscript apart at the appropriate places with long scissors and then use the glue to paste them into a new position on fresh sheets of paper.

Sometimes I had to draw lines and arrows to make the new sequence of paragraphs and sentences clear. By the end of this process, the manuscript looked like a mad scientist's art project.

I don't want to go back to that era. I love the tools we have for writing now. In your own creative work, you've probably experienced a similar kind of evolution of the tools you use.

But it really doesn't matter whether you write with a pen and a journal—the method I prefer for freewriting—with a PC, on your smartphone, via dictation software, with a quill pen, or by scratching words on a wall with a piece of charcoal. Pens, PCs, and smartphones don't create *anything*—you do. You are the creator no matter what tools you use.

So, it makes sense to find the tools that make your work flow and intrude the least into your creative process. Although some kinds of work rely on human-machine interaction, for the rest of us, the choice is subjective.

As a writer, I can report having done creative work by the following means:

- By hand, with pens and pencils, and in journals of many kinds

Meeting the Muse

- On manual typewriters, starting when I learned to type as a teenager
- On electric typewriters like the IBM Selectric
- On typesetting equipment I owned or had access to
- On word-processing workstations
- On early computers such as the Apple II and Compaq Deskpro
- On a whole host of modern Apple computers

If I separate the creative part of my work from the "production" part, then the devices become irrelevant because the real work of writing isn't done with our hands but with our heads and hearts. Sure, the modern software we have makes editing and other production-oriented tasks much faster, easier, and more enjoyable than wrestling with those glue pots, but the creative part remains the same.

So don't get hung up on the thought "If only I had . . . [a great fountain pen, new software, the absolutely perfect desk], then I'd be able to write!" Just get down to work with what you have. Getting in touch with your creativity, no matter what tool you are using, is a far better use of your time and energy than worrying about what you don't have.

> For me, inspiration comes from a bunch of places: desperation, deadlines.... A lot of times ideas will turn up when you're doing something else. And, most of all, ideas come from confluence—they come from two things flowing together. They come, essentially, from daydreaming.
>
> **—NEIL GAIMAN**

16

Inspiration is beautiful but overrated. Persistence is at least as important as inspiration, especially if you aspire to be a professional.

MANY ASPIRING CREATIVES THINK they need to wait for inspiration to truly be creative. People who never get around to creating anything—but who are convinced they will someday create something truly memorable—also fall for the idea they are just waiting for a magical moment of inspiration to arrive.

Stories from history promote this idea. For instance, Rainer Maria Rilke, an Austrian poet and novelist, completed the *Duino Elegies*, his most famous work (and some of the most beautiful and transformational poetry in the German language), in one burst of creativity lasting a few weeks. He described how he wrote in this period "with a sudden, renewed inspiration—writing in a frantic pace he described as a 'boundless storm, a hurricane of the spirit.'"[3]

And hey, it's great when it happens. But for most of us, and for most of the creative work we do, steady persistence is much more likely to bring us results than just sitting around waiting for a lightning bolt to strike while we're poised at our computers. Albert Einstein reportedly claimed that he was no smarter than his colleagues but that he worked at problems far longer than anyone else.

Many moments of inspiration will be completely unrelated to your work environment. You might be inspired while taking a shower, driving the kids to school, or staring at the acoustic tiles in your dentist's office—at any one of those quotidian moments that happen all the time when we're paying attention to something else. That's when inspiration will sneak up on you.

Then you can make use of these seeds of inspiration during your "work" time. Like a gardener, you can tend your ideas, water them with connections to other ideas, prop them up with stakes that will hold them until they are strong enough to stand on their own.

Meeting the Muse

Professionals are people who show up to do their job every day. What does that mean? If you're a writer, you show up every day, sit down, and write. Perhaps what you'll write today won't be very good. Or it may be wondrous. That's not our concern. If you show up, you affirm that writers are people who write, and if you keep doing it every day and pay attention, you'll get better as you go along.

If you're a painter, you paint. If you're a musician, you make music. Professionals can't afford to wait for inspiration. As someone said, you might find money in the street, but you can't live on it, can you?

Be a professional. Show up and get your work done. It's the basis for everything you will do.

You are the gardener of your own ideas, and these are the ideas that will populate the works you will be known by. Sticking with them, making something substantial from a momentary insight through your own hard work, is how you become your own Einstein.

Joel Friedlander

> You, the artist, you're not the puppet of the piano, you're not the puppet of the muse, but you're not its master, either. It's a relationship, it's a conversation, and all it wants is to be treated with respect and dignity—and it will return ten thousand times over.
>
> **—ELIZABETH GILBERT**

17

Most of the models we have of creative artists at work are media depictions designed to appeal to our fantasies. Creativity rarely looks the way you think it will.

THE WHOLE POINT OF creative inspiration is that it is completely new in some way; it can't be scheduled or anticipated. As creatives, our job is to show up for work every day, put in the day's work, and let inspiration take care of itself.

Before inspiration appears, we don't know what our new work will be or what path we'll be traveling to arrive there. It might be the one we least expected or a path we couldn't have imagined at all.

Are we capable of saying what form our creation should take? Since we are more like vessels for the transmission of new ideas, it follows that we can't necessarily dictate the form.

Just look at the unbelievable variety of creative expression surrounding us. Even an hour spent on YouTube will convince anyone of the abundant beauty, silliness, violence, chaos, profundity, hate, light, dark, and everything in between happening all the time in this roiling stew we call reality.

So, what does creation itself look like? If you're a writer, does it mean you must conform to some stereotype from an earlier time? Do you have to live in an attic, scrounge for money, and get rejected hundreds of times?

I think writers today look quite different from one another in a spectacular number of ways. A writer could be a young mom who works on drafts in her car while the kids are at soccer practice, or a lawyer who gets up an hour early every morning to work on his novel. Think of J. K. Rowling, writing *Harry Potter and the Philosopher's Stone* (which you may know as *Harry Potter and the Sorcerer's Stone*) in a café in Edinburgh while her baby slept by her side.

Meeting the Muse

Many writers have had similar, asymmetric lives: part creative professional and part ordinary citizen. But the media portrayals of creativity are so powerful, it's important to remember that only you determine what your creative life is like, no one else.

This realization eliminates the need to slavishly obey the voices in your head telling you that you should look or act like Philip Seymour Hoffman and Nicole Kidman when they played authors Truman Capote and Virginia Woolf. At the same time, it means that your creative life is your responsibility—and yours alone.

That's both frightening and exciting at the same time. It's frightening because when you're in the process of becoming the artist you want to be, you are operating without any external references to let you know whether you're on an authentic course or flailing in uncertainty. It's exciting because you know that when you finally arrive, you will be fully yourself, idiosyncratic in the best way, and authentically you.

That's worth a lot, no matter how long it takes to get there.

> See the rules. Keep most of them. Break one or two. But break them, don't bend them.
>
> **—SETH GODIN**

18

Nothing is more common than a good idea, yet nothing is more satisfying than a good idea transformed from a possibility into reality.

BEING BOWLED OVER BY the ingenuity, the originality, the brilliance of our own creative ideas is easy. It's fun to think of new things, stuff that seems so different, outrageous, or inventive it would *have to* make a huge splash in the world.

But ideas alone are rarely of much use in the world. A long and sometimes treacherous road runs from the original idea to the endpoint of seeing it become real.

Traveling this road requires persistence, perseverance, invention, accommodation—and maybe even a team—to bring your great idea into being.

Don't believe for a minute I'm immune to "idea euphoria" just because I can write about it.

Many years ago, I had a brainstorm: suppose I could hook up an electrical timer to my cassette player. (This is a machine from the ancient world that played digital recordings on magnetic tape spooled inside small plastic boxes.) It would wake me up with the music I liked the most, instead of the buzz of an alarm or the chatter of the radio, which were the only options available at a time when the consumer electronics business was in its infancy.

But did I have the ability to create a consumer electronics product? Did I know anything about manufacturing, distribution, or sales of such products? Did I even know anyone who could help? No, no, and no.

Before long, manufacturers began combining cassette players with early clock radios, and soon people were waking up to their favorite music. Did I have a good idea, or was it just a consumer's intuition about where the market would head next?

Then there was the time I realized shipping book proofs all over the country was a waste of energy and

Meeting the Muse

resources. Paper is heavy and expensive to ship. Wouldn't it be better to create a networked service that could send your PDF file—which costs nothing to ship—to where the printout was needed and then print it at a terminal near the person you were shipping it to? But again, I had no way of making this idea a reality, even though it solved a real problem.

Soon enough, Kinko's Copy Shops (now FedEx Office) set up such a network, and we no longer needed to ship hundreds of pages of paper. We now simply send a file and have it printed and picked up locally, no shipping needed.

I could tell you more stories—like the time I thought I could start a book club for people interested in spiritual literature (no, I couldn't). Or how I was going to bring together an entire community of people studying the same ideas, despite their hostility toward one another (no, I didn't). My point is, we shouldn't get intoxicated by the brilliance of our ideas without any thought of how—or whether—those ideas could be executed.

Now I'm much more productive because although I have lots of wild and crazy ideas, I tend to put the most effort into the ones that will have a practical outcome, where I can see a clear path between idea and realization.

Joel Friedlander

Stay with your work; it will pay off in the end. This is a long game.

> Creation is really a sustained period of bliss—even though the subject can still be very sad. Because there's the triumph of coming through and understanding that you have, and that you did it the way only you could do it—you didn't do it the way somebody told you to do it. You did it just the way you had to do it. And that is what makes us us.
>
> **—ALICE WALKER**

19

Anyone can imagine doing something extraordinary. Actually taking steps to achieve your vision is what sets you apart.

So often, we think we can't achieve something, or others can do it better than we could ever hope. It's a goal that's seemingly impossible to reach.

The problem may be that we are envisioning an already-finished product. From this vantage point, we don't see all the work and planning that went into making it. It can look so monumental that it's hard to even imagine where we would begin to try to create something as big and as impressive by ourselves.

But looked at from another point of view, even big, towering works might well be reachable. And a simple method can help you get started.

In your mind, look at the thing you want to produce, or look at a real-life example. Note the parts that make up the whole. Try to deconstruct the work in question to see what elements contributed to the eventual outcome.

For instance, a few years ago I realized that a training course would allow me to reach more authors with information about self-publishing than the number of people I could reach by just writing articles and posting them to my blog. But when I looked at the training courses I liked and used myself, I was overwhelmed with how big a task it was. How could I get from where I was—with nothing, basically—to having one of these polished, good-looking courses hosted on a secure site, with payment gateways and site security to keep nonmembers out? It all looked complicated and opaque from the outside.

Although the task seemed impossible, here's where breaking it down came to my rescue. Instead of stressing about how hard it would be to create everything on my own, I started looking at the specific steps I would need to take: I would need to make up a curriculum; create a name and brand for the course; figure out whether to offer video, audio, text, or some combination; and figure out how membership sites worked.

Gradually, over a period of about six months, I worked on these steps one at a time. I learned how to put together an effective lesson. Then I learned how to set up a membership site by researching and installing software that controlled access to the lessons in the course. Another task was figuring out how to create different kinds of "Buy" buttons for people to use.

Each of these tasks on its own was very doable; none of it was beyond me. Eventually, after putting all the pieces together, I was able to launch a finished training course with everything done, polished, and in working order. Amazing.

I've found this process works in other ways, too. Looking at a photo of beautiful Italian biscotti, you might ask, How the heck do you make those? But isn't a recipe simply another way to break down a process into simple, sequential steps? You could do it, too!

Do you want to create an article that gets dozens or hundreds of comments and backlinks from other sites? Study the ones attracting that kind of engagement, and then create your own version that's just a little bit better—one that contains more useful information, is presented in a more helpful or delightful way, or is more up to date—and you stand a good chance of getting the same kind of response.

This is also the secret behind many effective training programs. Would you like to create a special effect for your book cover, one that you've seen on covers from big publishers but that seems out of reach for your graphics skills? Free tutorials from bloggers or manufacturers or paid services (like the instructional programs on e-learning sites) will give you a step-by-step "recipe" that will show you exactly how to achieve the result you're looking for.

No matter what you want to create, the message is this: don't be intimidated by the finished products you see elsewhere. Instead, break down the steps it would take to get that result, and then start putting them into action.

Taking action will separate you from others who might also want to create the same kinds of things but who never consider trying to take those actions because they are unwilling or afraid or simply intimidated at the prospect.

You can do it—one step at a time.

Meeting the Muse

> Every moment can be a creative moment. For instance, as I type this I'm sitting in Starbucks, I have my phone set up on a mini-tripod taking a time-lapse of a beautiful sunrise. I realized that even the most mundane and ordinary moments of my day can be filled with moments of creativity.
>
> **—DAN BLANK**

20

What stimulates your own creativity? Own that.

As a child, I was a daydreamer, and this tendency has stayed with me throughout my life. A long, hot shower will put me in a trancelike state, and many of the ideas that get actualized in my work originated in a similarly loose, unfettered mental state.

My colleague Joan Stewart tells me her creativity is spurred by being around water. Any exposure to water will do, and Joan has found that when she needs creative inspiration, even washing the dishes will stimulate her.

Water is also a creative trigger for me as it is for many people, and I've loved being in the water and around the water since childhood. Jill and I have always lived near

Meeting the Muse

one shore or another. Even before I met Jill, most of my life had been spent near one coast or another. I was a competitive swimmer in high school and always enjoy a long, lazy session in a pool somewhere. I'm also a lifetime exerciser, and at one time I became a lap swimmer, spending hours over the years—in all seasons—slowly sliding through the water, stroking up and down the lanes of an outdoor pool nearby. You'd be amazed at the kinds of ideas you can have during an activity like this.

Anything you do regularly, especially in a formalized way, can become a *practice*, a way of layering another level of meaning into an otherwise ordinary activity. In this case, the meaning comes from doing the practice as a way to contact your inner creativity. For example, swimming for thirty minutes at a time, once your body knows how to do it, becomes a chance to have "long thoughts," to really explore an idea, an event, or a plan with the time and space to probe and reflect.

Years after I stopped lap swimming, I took up mountain biking, an "extreme" sport with a public reputation of attracting testosterone-driven young men taking big risks, although in fact all sorts of people and families are involved in this sport. I soon realized that unlike most of the riders I knew, my favorite activity was going on long uphill climbs, especially the climb up Mount Tamalpais, which starts in Mill Valley.

Tracing a long, winding path all the way up this mountain to its peak at 2,572 feet is a wide fire road that's perfect for biking. It was originally built for a railroad carrying visitors to the top of the mountain for the breathtaking views, but the tracks were pulled up long ago, leaving dirt and rock in their place.

Because it was built for a railroad, the road was graded carefully to an eight-degree incline, perfect for trains. This also turns out to be perfect for old guys like me riding mountain bikes. Once on the fire road, I experiment until I find the perfect gear to steadily climb while maintaining my ability to keep breathing since the whole trip up takes about an hour and forty minutes.

Often on these rides I drop into yet another trance-like state. Of course, I need to be quite a bit more attentive riding up a mountain on a bike than I do when I'm daydreaming in the shower.

What could you do for an hour and forty minutes in a meditative state? You could have more of those long thoughts, the kind you rarely have time for in the ordinary rush of life. You could work on a thorny problem you haven't been able to solve. Or you just might open

Meeting the Muse

yourself to the unending flow of ideas at the core of your creative engine.

Some creatives use music as a stimulus for creativity. For instance, author and opera singer R. S. Mollison described in an article the detailed playlists she listens to while writing various types of scenes for her novels.[4]

Other creatives use dream journals, take long walks in nature, engage in scrapbooking, or use cooking to stimulate their creativity. A half hour spent kneading a big ball of dough can be very productive, believe me.

And be prepared to be surprised. I spent over a year writing almost daily while sitting in my car. I had an iPad with a wireless keyboard, and I'd find an inconspicuous place to park, somewhere with a pleasant view on the other side of my windshield. Something about the quiet inside the car—being isolated and insulated yet able to observe the world outside—allowed me to create some of my best writing. No distractions, a window available for the occasional break from tapping the keyboard—it was perfect.

Whatever it is, finding out what stimulates your creativity will help you for years to come. Try sitting at a potter's wheel, jogging, or anything else that breaks the routine of the day, letting something new arise to surprise and delight you.

> Talent is insignificant. I know a lot of talented ruins. Beyond talent lie all the usual words: discipline, love, luck, but most of all, endurance.
>
> **—JAMES BALDWIN**

21

You have an unending stream of creativity running underground. All you have to do is find it.

We often refer to "tapping into" our creativity, as if it's stored in an underground reservoir. Of course, we're referring to a place inside us but below the level of our ordinary awareness.

At this point we might notice the way we talk about what's going on inside us is very odd. For instance, we frequently make the distinction between certain actions we consider conscious and others that are unconscious. Psychologists and brain researchers tell us only a very small fraction of our total mental activity is in the conscious category. The rest, being unconscious, is mostly unavailable to us.

This comes as a surprise to many people. If it's true, then the thoughts, feelings, desires, plans, memories, arguments, inventions, and everything else crowding our minds are just a small bit of everything going on inside us; we simply can't see it.

Which leads one to wonder, What is all this unknown activity, and how could it be going on without my knowing about it? Our discomfort with this unknown *and unknowable* region of our own awareness may come from realizing we exercise no control over this vast internal realm.

As we grow up, we are subtly introduced to the ideas that we need to be in control, everything is knowable, and we must be the "masters of our domain." At some point, if you've been paying attention, you inevitably come to understand that most of our mental faculties aren't under our control, they are unknowable, and we have, in effect, no mastery at all over our own minds.

This really came home to me during freewriting. When I first learned freewriting, I had to trust that an internal process of some kind would spring into action to populate the empty pages of my notebook—with something. But what that something would be, and where it would come from, I had no idea.

One thing Suzanne Murray often said to her freewriting students was, "No surprise for the writer; no surprise for the reader." She meant we might write things with no antecedents, things completely unrelated to the content of our conscious minds, things that might surprise or even shock us as we wrote them.

In freewriting, you might start off in the room with the other writers but soon find yourself in ancient Greece or on an imaginary planet or inside the mind of a Labrador retriever. One minute you're writing your prompt over and over, waiting for something to happen, and the next moment a whole scene, remembered or imagined, appears and starts pouring out of you in a great rush.

Where do you think all that invention comes from if not your unconscious mind?

Because of the way this exercise works, every freewriting session became an incredible journey of discovery. It turned out letting go of the editing and judging that usually go on in my head while writing was incredibly powerful. Unhooking the inner judge in an attempt to allow whatever came up—regardless of how odd, crazy, unsettling, disturbing, or off-the-wall it might be—to be expressed, to keep saying yes to whatever came to mind, is what led me directly to the creative source within me. When I made room for my unconscious to participate, it never failed to appear.

This ability to connect to your own stream of unending creativity will give you a confidence you've never had before and provide you with a source you can return to over and over, surprising yourself and, eventually, a whole world of readers.

> Creativity is just connecting things. When you ask creative people how they did something, they feel a little guilty because they didn't really do it, they just saw something. It seemed obvious to them after a while.
>
> **—STEVE JOBS**

22

When you meet your muse, she may not look the way you imagined. No matter what, embrace your muse.

The hallway is long and dark, lit by torches whose light flickers on the stone walls, dark shadows obscuring as much as the flames illuminate. At the end of the hall, a hulking wooden door.

As I approach the door, I see it's banded with iron plates, rugged from wear over uncounted centuries.

The door is also ajar and, as I near it, it slowly swings open.

A not-very-young brunette in long white robes sits perched on a stool, idly flipping the pages of a magazine. She's wearing running shoes with the laces dangling, untied. Her hair's a bit mussed, but she seems like someone with a lot of time on her hands and not a lot of patience.

"Well, hello," she says as I stand, star-struck, in the doorway.

And so it begins.

* * *

This scene isn't from a novel I'm writing. It's the record of my first meeting with my muse during a freewriting session years ago.

Yes, I met her by writing about her, marveling as the entire scene appeared on the page in front of me. It was so vivid I could feel the dank air in that hallway, smell the history of the old stones lining the walls, hear the soft footfalls as I made my way along.

What's a muse? A force (usually presented as a woman) that is the source of inspiration for a creative artist.

There's no requirement for creatives to find a muse, but if you do, you will have a powerful ally on the long journey of coming into yourself as an artist. Your muse can give you the confidence you need to keep moving forward on a project you might have doubts about or one that's very risky. I've found the muse best at answering sincere questions, whether they have to do with what I'm writing or some project only beginning to take shape in my mind.

The muse is a sounding board for your ideas, where your own creative genius can bounce new ideas off a receptive *other* for your own benefit. You might think this is just talking to yourself, but you would be wrong. Why? Remember, the part of our minds we know and have some influence over is only a very small part of all the activity going on inside us.

So, talking to yourself involves your conscious mind creating both sides of a conversation. This isn't so different from the way we talk to ourselves in everyday life.

But if your conscious mind opens a means of communication with your unconscious, you can't really claim to be talking to yourself because what's in your unconscious isn't what we think of as "ourselves." What's in there is completely unknown, foreign to our usual ways of thinking about ourselves.

Now keep in mind that when you find your muse, it won't look or act like mine. Writers have reported disappointment when their muse first appeared. One writer told me her muse was a large fellow with a huge beer gut who looked like a plumber. Another said her muse was a large black crow, a bird she found unattractive.

And you never know where your muse will appear. A novelist told me his muse appeared as one of the characters in the book he was working on and guided him throughout the writing.

Maybe you'll discover a unique muse for every book you write or a different muse for different types of creative work. Or maybe, like me, you'll keep going back to the same source.

Does it matter? Not really. The muse is a doorway, a connection you make to all the things you know but *don't know you know*. Some of these things reside in our shared cultural memory; others are likely an inheritance from generations of our ancestors' DNA. I have no idea, really, but I want to open that door, don't you?

In any event, you can't fight how your muse makes its appearance because your job is not to *create* your muse but to try to *discover* it. If your muse looks like a plumber or a crow or a charming young woman, it's all the same.

And you might be surprised to find out the muse can be a pretty tough cookie. She might not like my latest idea, and she has no hesitation in pointing out just how difficult it might be to bring it to completion. Or she might remind me of other harebrained schemes I've had in the past, ones that ultimately failed.

Meeting the Muse

On the other hand, I've mostly been supported by my muse. She's full of ideas I could never have come up with myself. She's always there, always willing to listen to a new proposal. She doesn't mince words when giving her opinions and, when the conversation is over, she dismisses me without a word, going back to her glossy magazine. That's my signal to retreat through the door and back down that long hall.

Over the years, I've come to treasure my walks down the long stony hallway with its heavy door at the end. The time I spend there, talking with the muse, is deeply enriching. My muse is both guide and mentor, jokester and fan, and if you find your own muse, I'm going to bet she never disappoints you.

> [Creativity is] just making something. It might be something crummy or awkward or not ready for prime time. If you make something, you are creative.
>
> **–SONIA SIMONE**

23

Everything has a natural history, and you'll find it in the fourth dimension.

CREATIVITY OFTEN INVOLVES GAINING insight into the world, seeing truths we can communicate through writing, a visual art, music, or some other expressive means. But the people and objects we see around us aren't static, trapped in the moment in which we see them. The key to understanding their history is *time*, commonly referred to as the "fourth dimension," after the three physical dimensions of length, width, and height.

For instance, I can describe a simple object by noting its physical dimensions, its color, weight, texture, and so on. This is all ordinary and normal. But does this

Meeting the Muse

physical description reflect the complexity and history of the object? Does it tell the whole story?

We can extend this physical inventory into entirely new dimensions in two ways, each of which holds tremendous promise.

Let's take a common object as an example. Right now, I'm writing at a table at a coffee shop. The table is a pretty typical example of a coffee shop table. It's about thirty inches tall with a heavy metal base and a central metal column that holds up a circular dark wood top about two feet across. Since I'm sitting in one location of a large national chain of coffee shops, the table was undoubtedly designed by someone for its precise purpose.

But where was the table born? Who created the metal parts, such as the stand and the column and the unseen bolts that likely hold it together? Was the wood shipped from a remote location in Canada? Were the rest of the parts preassembled in Asia?

From my vantage point, I have no way of knowing how this object was designed and produced and ended up here, underneath my laptop. But, like all objects, it has its own natural history that in some ways defines it as much as it is defined by its physical properties.

This is the first way we can apply the fourth dimension to our understanding of the table: we can trace its history in time from conception to the present moment.

The second way is to imagine the future of the table. As long as it performs the function its current owners need it for, and as long as it matches the decor of the coffee shop, it will likely continue its current role.

When it starts to wobble, someone may try to fix it. If it gets scratched or banged up, it may be refinished.

At some point, however, it will no longer perform the function it was acquired to perform. Then it might get sold, along with a lot of other used coffee shop furniture, and go on to another role somewhere else.

Many times, you don't have to supply much imagination to see the natural history of an object. When we lived in New York City, I enjoyed occasional visits to the Argosy Book Store on East Fifty-Ninth Street. The store is packed with six narrow floors of rare books, maps, and other collectibles. You can easily lose yourself for an hour or so just wandering around, enjoying the fruits of earlier generations.

One day, Jill and I saw a wooden bookcase on the street near our home on the Upper West Side sporting a decal that read, "Argosy Book Store." This is very normal in Manhattan, where people put furniture they no

Meeting the Muse

longer want on the street knowing there's a good chance someone else will have a use for it and haul it away for them. In New York, it's a system that works.

We needed a bookcase, so we carted it a block or two to our apartment, cleaned it up, and used it for books.

When we moved to California, we brought the bookcase with us and it became part of our infant son's room. To match the decor, we painted it with a bright blue glossy paint. Later, I added brackets to the back of the bookcase to attach it to the wall, something necessary only if you live in an area where earthquakes happen every once in a while.

When my son grew up and moved on to university, Jill reclaimed the bookcase to use for her growing library of books she's accumulated over the years. It sits today, still blue, in our bedroom.

What is the natural history of this bookcase? When I look at it, if I pay attention, I can see the hand of whoever designed it; the way the shelves tilt just slightly to keep the books more secure, the way the sharp corners have been gently rounded.

But in my mind, I also see it sitting on the street in Manhattan where we picked it up. I think about the thousands of people who must have stopped to take a book off the shelf while it was on duty at Argosy Book

Store, as well as the many children's books and toys cluttering the shelves while my son grew up.

And it's not too hard to imagine what might eventually happen to it. It could be sold for a few dollars at a garage sale when we don't need it, or it might be tipped off the back of my SUV at the local dump if we can't find another way to get rid of it.

This long view of the bookcase describes what some people call its time body, the shape it would trace if you could observe it through the time that describes its long history.

This effort alone—seeing objects in their fourth dimension—opens incredible possibilities for the creative mind, but we're not quite finished yet.

Let me ask you a couple of questions about this bookcase. What if we found out the wood it was made of had been farmed with slave labor? What if the lacquer used to protect the bookcase contained toxic chemicals and caused severe health consequences for the workers who finished the bookcase and other wooden items made for export?

Of course, it's equally possible the bookcase was made in a small workshop by dedicated woodworkers who had ownership of their factory, took great pride in their work, and tried to make their environment as safe

Meeting the Muse

and as humane as possible. Might these circumstances have imbued the bookcase with certain properties, even though we may not have the sensitivity or the instruments to measure such differences directly?

Long ago I studied the work of Peter Ouspensky, a Russian philosopher who claimed the history of objects does in fact become imbued in the objects themselves. He said if we had the sensitivity or could build instruments to measure such things, we would see a huge difference between a brick coming from the wall of a church and an apparently identical brick taken from the wall of a prison.

Tuning in to the natural history of objects—or of people—can have a profound effect on how we approach the world. Knowing their backstory and being able to intuit something about their future gives us a whole different relation to time—and our place in it—than we had before. As a stimulus to creativity, this profound effect can have wide-ranging consequences for you as an artist.

Look around you. The world is not so simple when you see it from the fourth dimension, is it?

Joel Friedlander

> What I capture in spite of myself interests me more than my own ideas.
>
> **—PABLO PICASSO**

24

Creativity can flourish in both freedom and constraint.

CREATIVITY CAN FLOURISH BOTH when it's free and when it's under constraints.

Let's say you have a job and you have to go to work from nine to five, you sit in a cubicle, and you have to attend meetings several times a week. That's potentially putting some serious constraints on your spontaneous creativity, isn't it?

I've had plenty of jobs with lots of constraints over the years. What you dream of when you're constrained like this is freedom so you don't have to be at any particular place at any specific time, you can take a day off, you can even be goofy if the spirit moves you to goofiness.

None of this is ordinarily allowed in such constrained settings.

When you do gain your freedom, it feels fantastic. You now feel as if you can unleash your creativity, do something new, break your usual patterns, make all sorts of things possible.

So you can see that the constraints you were under, in a sense, created the feeling of freedom you experience when the constraints are loosened. In other words, if you hadn't been constrained, you wouldn't have had the creative release when granted your freedom.

On the other side, if you are completely free and can do anything you want, adopting some voluntary constraints can open new creative avenues for you.

If you're a writer, you might be surprised how adopting the formalized constraints of a new form can take your work into remarkable new places. One of the easiest ways to experience this is to try writing in a form that imposes strict constraints on the writer. For example, if you love the sonnets of William Shakespeare, you could try your hand at the same form he used.

These sonnets are generally written in *iambic pentameter*, a term that describes the rhythm and length of each line. In short, *iambs* are sets of two syllables, with the emphasis on the second syllable. The word *pentameter* tells us there are five of these pairs, meaning each line has ten syllables in total.

If you read this line from Shakespeare's twelfth sonnet and emphasize the italicized syllables, you'll see exactly how this translates into poetry:

When *I* do *count* the *clock* that *tells* the *time*

You can also appreciate how the simple, short words the poet used create a kind of syncopation, reminding us of the ticking of the clock. Very artful.

Sonnets also have a set rhyming pattern and a set number of lines, and each sonnet ends with two lines that rhyme.

Writing a sonnet takes a bit of practice, but it's not out of the reach of any competent writer. If you've never tried to write within a form like this, it's well worth your while to experiment because you might find something entirely new.

Perhaps an easier experiment would be writing a haiku, the short form of Japanese poetry. See "Write a Haiku" in the exercise section for more on this.

Constraints themselves force you into a creative mode where you can rise to meet the imperatives of the form. Finding just the right word to fit the poem, the syllable count, and the imagery you are creating can be difficult.

These forms are very conventional, and that's okay. You can also develop new forms, but learning to operate within the existing forms has a lot of advantages because they contain the history of all the other artists who have come before you and who wrote in the same form.

When you write sonnets, you have Shakespeare and all the other sonnet writers to learn from and compare. With haiku, almost as old as the sonnet, you have examples dating back to the seventeenth century. This long history is what established these forms as conventions in the first place.

Freedom and constraints. They are not right and wrong but two sides of the same coin. Remember, the constraints often are responsible for the freedom we experience, and we can often experience both during our creative journey.

You can't use up creativity. The more you use, the more you have.

—MAYA ANGELOU

25

Telling the winners from the losers can take a long time.

IDEAS HAPPEN IN A flash—always. I might be scraping the grill clean on a warm day at the beginning of summer or daydreaming in the hot embrace of the shower when a thought streaks across my mind.

Zounds! is my stunned response. *I never thought of that before!* But this new thing—a character, a scene, a workflow, a process, a strategy, an idea for a product—completely captivates me.

I'm intoxicated by the newness of this thing, the fact no one else has thought of it. I start to see in my mind how I will bring it to life. Of course, this pleasantly fuzzy daydream skips right over the planning, estimating, networking, and all the other work required to make it a reality. No, at first there are no obstacles, no unforeseen glitches—it's all smooth sailing. It's going to be fantastic, profitable, earth-shattering, or plot advancing—whatever the case may be.

But creatives soon learn that not every impulse—no matter how brilliant it seems at first—is destined to see the light of day. Once you look at the details, you realize your initial thought was missing pieces—pieces that perhaps don't even exist—or elements that, if added to the original concept, would radically change the cost, effectiveness, or purpose of your lovely idea.

Believing in your own creativity means you're going to have more ideas over your lifetime than you will ever be able to actualize. Some of these ideas must be sacrificed so that others may live. You are both the originator *and* the executioner in the economy of creative action.

Sometimes, you might need to abandon ideas you hold dear because prioritizing the time you have to work on your creative projects puts serious limits on what you can afford to take on. In other cases, you may come to realize you don't have the specific skills, the necessary training, or the connections in the market to make some of your ideas work. You might simply shelve some of

Meeting the Muse

these ideas for a later time when you're in a better position to take advantage of them.

This has happened to me repeatedly over the years. Back in 2010, I had the brainstorm that I could help lots of authors by creating templates that would eliminate the need to hire a book designer to typeset and lay out their books.

Did I act on that idea? I tried to find someone to help with the technical side of the project, but the people I found eventually fizzled out. I shelved the project because I couldn't move ahead.

Two years later, almost by chance, I made the acquaintance of Tracy Atkins, a writer and technologist who was commenting on my blog articles. I gradually realized he was the perfect person to put this idea of mine into practice to see if it would work. Within a few months, we had launched a business based on this idea, a business that has been profitable from the first day.

In 2011, I started making notes for a "Book Launch Toolkit" to guide new authors through the ordeal of launching their books. I had a pretty good idea of what it would be like, but I didn't act on it. I lacked the time, and I didn't have a marketing platform or means of delivery, so it looked like an impractical idea and I put it aside.

Almost five years later I dug out my notes and, with the help of blogger Kimberly Grabas, finally put together this groundbreaking product. Why did it take so long? By 2015 I had acquired what I had been lacking in 2011: a mailing list of authors, which gave me a platform from which to market the product; the ability to network with an enthusiastic partner; and the technology my partner and I had established for doing e-commerce online.

In both cases, it took years before the conditions were right to move forward. Until then, I didn't know if these ideas were winners or losers.

And so it goes. Learning how to ditch the losers, accelerate the winners, and identify the slow bloomers needing months or years to come to fruition is part of the life and work of writers, artists, creative engineers, and others whose work fosters an ongoing relationship with their own creativity and who are able to move the results of their creativity into the world.

> The cutting of the gem has to be finished before you can see whether it shines.
>
> **—LEONARD COHEN**

26

Consider your life and death.

THIS MAY SEEM LIKE an odd topic for a book on creativity, but if the subject of your own death doesn't make you too uncomfortable, it can supercharge your creative output. Of course, you'll need to put aside for a few minutes your fear of death and your aversion to the whole subject. I know it's not easy, but we have a lot to gain, so give it a try.

Think about this: everything that dies must have been born first, because if something isn't alive, it can't die. Only living things experience death.

From this point of view, you can see that just the fact of being born means, inevitably, you're going to die. Nothing is wrong or surprising about this; it's a fact of life for all living things, from a mayfly with a life expectancy of five minutes to a bristlecone pine living for five thousand years. What all living things have in common is their impermanence. As certainly as you are alive today, reading this, your time of living will come to an end, as it has for all those who have come before you.

We have two opposing ideas here because there's a bright line between being alive and not being alive. Our ability to keep two opposing ideas like these in our minds at the same time, while realizing each is true in its own way, is one way to describe a dynamic tension that inspires creation.

Dualities like this are all around us. For example, a writer, while crafting a scene in his novel is, in his mind, inside the world he is creating, mingling with his characters, experiencing the drama and detail of their world. At the same time, he's still in a world of physical reality, sitting at his desk in the living room. He holds both of these realities within him at the same time, although the two worlds cannot meet.

In the same way, we can be poised between the two incompatible realities of life and death. On the one hand, we have the fullness of life in all its unknowable complexity and delight. On the other hand, we have the opposite: nothing, a void, an abyss.

Meeting the Muse

At the juncture of these two worlds is a dynamism in which you can live with both worlds in your awareness at the same time. You can get out of bed, get ready for the day, and then attend to your work, all the while mindful of the "ultimate reality" imbuing life with its own meaning. You can seek the counsel offered by death—even by your own death.

The practice of considering your own death is an old one. The skulls you see in oil paintings from previous eras are there because a human skull acts as a *memento mori*, a reminder of one's own mortality. The guarantee that our time is limited—and what we do with this fact—is inherent in much of our creative activity.

Do you want to leave something behind when you depart this world? Do you have trouble prioritizing your work, deciding what's more important and what's less so? Contemplating the arc of your life can help.

Although for most of our lives our remaining years seem to stretch toward an always-distant horizon, the fact is, each of us has a specific amount of time here. We just don't know how much. But when you understand this, you realize every hour you "spend" is deducted from a specific time allotment.

Many years ago, as a young man, I belonged to a group practicing a philosophical system with the promise it would help me "realize my own potential." At one group meeting, the leader talked about the inevitability of death. While sitting quietly, listening attentively in a back row, I suddenly had a perfectly clear vision of myself *after* death. I saw my body lying lifeless on the ground. It was shocking but not unexpected. What did I think my dead body would look like?

This vision persists in my memory, even forty-odd years afterward, popping into my awareness at random times. Rather than being disturbing, it always has a calming effect on me. My own death, through these moments, has become a wise counselor, helping me put in perspective the ups and downs of daily life. Successes and failures take on a different meaning in light of this vision of me, lying inert and finished on the ground. The work I will be able to leave behind looms far larger by comparison.

You don't have to be morbid, unless that's part of your shtick. But I find the regular practice of standing up straight, looking at myself, and acknowledging my personal march toward decrepitude and death to be a worthwhile endeavor. It heightens my appreciation of the world—and after all, that's at the core of why I create—giving it a depth and complexity that it wouldn't otherwise have.

Try it. Then go watch a cat video.

> The most beautiful times of day are dawn
> and dusk when shadows are long, offering
> contrast, refuge and form. Death is the shadow
> that gives shape to existence, urgency to love,
> brilliance to life.
>
> **—ROGER COHEN**

27

Quiet your mind, and you'll be surprised at how creative you become.

Have you noticed the endless chatter going on inside your mind? The long-running audio track to your life, the one no one can hear but you? All those voices inside your head—your mother, your husband, Mrs. Smith from third grade—with advice, comments, criticism, confusion, and judgment about every little thing you're doing as you're doing it?

In some circles, this phenomenon is called "monkey mind" due to its endless and mostly meaningless jabbering. Spiritual practitioners have been trying to get a grip on this problem for millennia, and all seekers who realize how their inner world is being dominated by mental

Meeting the Muse

"static" must wrestle with this situation right from the beginning of their work on themselves.

But this situation is equally critical to creative workers. Certainly, many of our most famous writers, artists, and musicians haven't explicitly talked about "quieting the mind," but perhaps they had an innate sense of how to get rid of the noise, to concentrate on what might arise from their own creative depths.

Whether or not William Shakespeare ever sat around meditating (and I doubt he did), learning how to use the equipment you were born with can never be a bad goal or have a disappointing outcome. So, I'd like to give you one of my favorite mental exercises of all time. This is an exercise I found many years ago, when I was first shown how to listen to my own brain instead of just stumbling along in blind obedience to those hectoring voices.

It relies on a trick of attention. Here's what I mean.

Sit quietly for a moment and see what happens. You may not have been aware of the voices in your head when you were active, but as soon as you quiet down, I bet you can hear them, and if you're at all like me, they might be saying things like this:

- "Why am I doing this?"
- "I wish I could get my blog updated."

- "There's a lot of stuff on my desk. I should clean up."
- "Oops, forgot that tax thing again. I'll need to do it today."

These are the thoughts that started erupting in my mind the moment I stopped writing. I view these as random signals, like papers blown up into the air on a windy city street or like messages flashing across a blank sky. The problem is, while all this talk is going on, it's hard to hear anything deeper, and harder still to connect to our creative source.

Here's my solution: learn the art of "active listening."

While these thoughts arise, unbidden, from a place we can't reach, we don't have to worry about the *content* of these thoughts at all. Instead we need to realize we have the power to change the situation. Although these voices seem to be going on without any involvement on our part, the fact is, we are listening to them.

Once you realize this, the next logical thought is, What would happen if I stopped listening? Now you've entered the realm of active listening. It's *active* because you choose what to listen to in your own mind. For instance, if I stop writing again, I can choose to pay attention to other sounds in my environment.

Right now, I could listen to the low rumbling of the hard drive in my computer as it does whatever it's doing next to me. Or I could listen to the steady but distant thrum of traffic or the muffled voices reaching me through the wall behind my desk.

It doesn't really matter. These environmental sounds are basically neutral and don't provoke any emotion. When you listen this way, you might find some sounds are more pleasant to you than others, but they all possess one thing in common: they have nothing to do with you.

I think you'll find settling into this space of active listening opens whole new worlds for you. It may sound insane, but believe me, this is really big.

The reason? The only time you can be actively listening to the world around you is in the present moment. This one fact guarantees if you learn this simple practice, you will change your level of awareness, possibly in life-changing ways.

Give it a try. Stop listening to those internal judgments, reprimands, reminders, and attacks. Free your mind from the junk of the past, bring it into the right-here, right-now world where your creative impulse—from the quiet of your mind—can break through with new insights, new perspectives, and new creative work.

Joel Friedlander

> A writer—and, I believe, generally all persons—must think that whatever happens to him or her is a resource. All things have been given to us for a purpose, and an artist must feel this more intensely. All that happens to us, including our humiliations, our misfortunes, our embarrassments, all is given to us as raw material, as clay, so that we may shape our art..
>
> **—JORGE LUIS BORGES**

28

Don't dictate to your creativity.

IN CREATIVE WORK, SOMETIMES we think we know what the outcome is going to be. Maybe you need another pattern design in purple to complete a series of color-coordinated patterns. But when you sit down, shake off the cobwebs, and try to get started, you find everything you're drawing wants to be a wild, iridescent green, not purple at all.

Why worry about the form your creativity wants to take? Is it your job to dictate terms? No, it's your job to pay attention, to flow with the creative impulse as it comes and not try to block or direct it.

In other words, don't be afraid to let go and see what happens. Remember, you're not really the "owner" of your creative thoughts, are you? None of us have any idea where these thoughts come from or why they arise inside us at all.

Understanding this in your own life can be incredibly liberating because if you don't own these thoughts, you have no responsibility for what they say or imagine, do you? This means you can let go of the inhibitions, fear, and uncertainty stopping you from saying what needs to be said, what *wants* to be said.

It's amazing how many of us are afraid of our own creativity. I know authors who have terrible, beautiful stories to tell, but they can't tell them because of this fear. It's because these authors believe their thoughts are who they are.

But a big part of the message in this little book is you don't have to hang on to that belief anymore. I'm not saying it will be easy or fast, but I know you can let go of your dogged but insane belief in your own thoughts. If you can let go even a little bit, it will have a profound effect on your creative life.

When you back away from this belief and start to see that your creativity comes from a source you cannot know and that will always remain a mystery, everything will change. Instead of stress and writer's block, you will find curiosity and delight at what is coming out of your pen, your brush, or your keyboard. How interesting!

How novel! So why try to dictate what form your creativity takes?

Consider Dr. Spencer Silver of 3M, who in 1968 was attempting to develop a superstrong adhesive but accidentally created an adhesive that was a complete failure. It was weak where it was supposed to be strong. But the odd thing was, it was *reusable*.

It was a normal experimental failure, but Arthur Fry, another scientist at 3M, supplied the creative spark, realizing this "error" was in fact very valuable. Thus was born the Post-it note.

Or how about Dr. Alexander Fleming, who in 1928 returned to his lab after a vacation and noticed that the mold that had grown on his experiments while he was gone had prevented the growth of bacteria. This was the birth of penicillin, an antibiotic that has been the savior of many millions of people. Because of Fleming's creative spark, he realized what was going on instead of just throwing all the moldy samples into the trash.

We creatives know all about the fickle nature of creativity. The little story you started that ends up being a chapter in a bruising novel of abuse and recovery. The draft after draft of an article that just won't come together no matter what we try. So many failures. Who said the life of a creative was all fun?

Joel Friedlander

I don't know how your creative life has evolved and if you even think about how it happened. For me, it gradually dawned on me I had become the servant, not the master, of my own creative impulse.

In the raw act of creation, I'm more of a stenographer, an interpreter of signs and signals that may not be apparent to anyone else, than I am the procreator, the point of origin for everything I produce. And you know what? That's fine with me.

> We do not know until the shell breaks what kind of egg we have been sitting on.
>
> **—T. S. ELIOT**

Conclusion
Go and create.

Are you busy? Me, too. But I'm a writer, which means I *write*. And to write, I have to find (or steal) time because it takes many hours to be creative and actually have something to show for it.

As a creative, it's up to you to take responsibility for your work. Nobody else can do this for you, and you shouldn't let anyone try. This means doing what's necessary to reach your creative goals.

Setting aside a regular time, having a place to practice your art, maintaining the discipline of real creative work—these are your tasks and your true joy.

In this book, I've tried to inspire you with the amazing and transcendent possibilities of creative thought and action. Were you inspired?

Then put something of yourself into the world. Go and create.

Flex-Your-Creativity Exercises

We've talked about many of the opportunities creativity brings us, as well as the obstacles that can stand in the way of reaching our creative goals.

The best way I know to bring the ideas in this book to life is to put them in practice.

In this section, you'll find exercises that can help you stimulate your own creativity. Some will appeal more than others, so follow your intuition to decide which to try first.

Throughout, remember that setting aside time to dive into the creative process often has an element of play, and I encourage you to enjoy this journey while you're on it. We start with the most basic of all exercises: Pay Attention.

Flex-Your-Creativity Exercises

∴ PAY ATTENTION ∴

If you long for inner quiet, allowing your most creative impulses to arise from deep within you, start to think about ways to be present in your own life. Here are some suggestions that have helped many people achieve the ability to drop into the present.

- *Stop.* The rush of everyday life seems endless. What if you just stopped right where you are? Creating a break like this from your ordinary patterns can open you up to things you may have rushed right past. Stop when you get out of your car in the parking lot. Stop right in the middle of loading the dryer. Stop anytime and see what's in that moment with you, see if you can feel the urge to keep moving forward. When you stop like this, for a moment you return to yourself, to the place where creativity abides.
- *Do the usual unusually.* Find a different route to work, even if it's only a little different. Maybe it will cost you an extra thirty seconds, but waking yourself from the slumber of routine will be worth it. After all, this is your one and only life. Don't you want to be present for it?

Flex-Your-Creativity Exercises

- *Notice things.* Try to be aware of yourself in whatever environment you find yourself. (By the way, this is also the ultimate cure for boredom.) No matter what place you're in right now, it's likely you haven't noticed *everything* about it. Be like a detective; everything is a clue, if you only know how to look at it the right way. My favorite way to do this is with the senses. Here are just a few examples:
  - Do you smell anything? Does the smell remind you of anything from your past? What's the connection?
  - What do you hear? All around us are sounds—buzzes, clicks, and myriad other noises we usually miss when we're paying more attention to the movie running in our heads or the thoughts taking up all our mental space.
  - Are you getting any "messages" from your body right now, any sensations you can isolate? How about the texture of the clothing you're wearing right now? What does your right foot feel like right now?
- *See yourself within the flow of time.* We are so committed to continuously moving forward, it can be a shock to enlarge our personal sense of time.

Flex-Your-Creativity Exercises

Wherever you are, turn around slowly. Now you're looking at the space you just left. Do you remember it, what you were feeling and thinking there? Are there traces you've left behind? What are all the decisions and accidents that led you to be here now? Where do you see yourself going from here?

Some people have called these practices ways of bringing yourself back to your own center. Would you like to try?

Flex-Your-Creativity Exercises

❖ PRACTICE FREEWRITING ❖

More than any other creative practice, freewriting liberated me from many years of being creatively stuck.

What is freewriting? It's a deceptively simple practice that taps into our creative potential. It starts with a very short list of ingredients and is guided by a few simple ideas.

Why would you want to use it?

- Freewriting liberates your writer's voice and connects you to the vibrant stream of creativity lying just under the surface of your ordinary thinking.
- Freewriting can be used to launch you right over a writer's block, to explore painful emotional memories, or to work out problems in a longer piece. I use it primarily to contact my unconscious.
- Freewriting is a simple, structured practice, flexible and forgiving. It can be used as the base of a regular writing practice, spontaneously whenever you want to go deeper into a subject, or as a group exercise with your writing partners.

When we freewrite, we try as much as possible to suspend judgment about what we are writing. This makes freewriting an exercise in getting out of our own

Flex-Your-Creativity Exercises

way. You may notice you are writing in a way you would usually find unacceptable or foreign.

You might find yourself expressing strong, alien, even violent stories or feelings. *Don't stop.* Try to simply observe the process rather than interrupt it. Marvel at the fact that, like Walt Whitman, we each "contain multitudes," many of whom we have yet to meet.

Here are my freewriting guidelines. However, in the spirit of freedom, feel free to not follow any that don't feel right to you.

- *Set a timer.* Having a reliable timer will free you from being drawn away from what you are writing to check the time. If you're in a good flow, you can continue writing after the time has expired until you complete your thought. For this exercise, set your timer for ten minutes. As soon as you hit the "Start" button, start writing and *don't stop writing* until the timer ends.

- *Use a prompt.* If you run out of ideas before the time is up, start writing the prompt instead. Very soon a new thought will arise, and you can start writing again. The most reliable prompt I've found is from Natalie Goldberg, author of *Writing Down the Bones,* among other books. Her simple statement "I remember" has been the basis for

Flex-Your-Creativity Exercises

countless freewrites and never disappoints. Many other prompts exist, of course, and you can use a photo or a piece of music or a painting as a prompt, too.

- *Keep your pen moving.* Again, don't stop writing until the timer goes off.
- *Write quickly.* Write a little bit faster than you can form your thoughts, even if it's uncomfortable. Messy handwriting is fine; words you can barely decipher are fine. Trust that what's important for you to unearth will make itself known to you at some point.
- *Use the first word.* Don't try to think of the perfect word, don't cross out or erase the word you wrote, just use the first word that comes to mind and go with it. Don't worry about paragraphing, subject-verb agreement, or even if what you are writing makes any sense at all. Don't worry about who will be offended by what you're writing or that it "doesn't sound like you." Just write.
- *Write garbage.* Give yourself permission to write a really bad first draft. You can always edit it later, but this permission allows you to do something new. Try to avoid any thoughts about what you are writing. You are just there to propel the pen—that's

Flex-Your-Creativity Exercises

your sole job. Telling yourself it's okay to write terrible first drafts is incredibly liberating. Try it.
- *Go for it.* If the first thing that pops into your mind is ridiculous, go for it. If it's violent, see where it goes. Be open to the unexpected. After all, you didn't create these thoughts, did you? Our job is to honor them and allow them to come to light.

If you think this won't work for you, please try it for a week. Pick a block of time you can set aside each day no matter what. You may need to get up earlier, watch a bit less television, shorten your lunch hour, or sit in your car while your child is in after-school activities.

How much time? Somewhere between ten minutes and two hours. Try ten minutes to get started. If possible, practice around the same time of day. Find a spot where you can be undisturbed, one that you can return to day after day as often as possible. This will set an intention within your mind and your body: this is your time to write.

For several years, I did this daily practice sitting in my car, writing in a journal or using an iPad with a keyboard. The key is to find what works for you.

Prepare to be amazed at what comes out of your pen and spills onto the page. You may be surprised, but remember, everything is coming from within you, and it will never stop.

Flex-Your-Creativity Exercises

❖ CREATE A LIST OF LISTS ❖

Lists—who can live without them? Lists are everywhere: the one I clutch in my hand while shopping, the list of system requirements on the outside of a box of software, the list of voter resolutions I'm asked to vote on at the ballot box, bullet points in a blog article. Lists are ubiquitous because they reflect our continued attempts to mentally organize ourselves.

Lists imply a hierarchy of some kind or a ranking of relevance: a list of countries ranked by per capita income, for example; standings of the baseball teams in the National League; stops I should make on the way home. Each imposes its own hierarchy, ordered by importance or sequence or some other logical arrangement.

Lists work because this is how we think, how we deal with all the information buffeting us every single day. Because lists reflect how we think, they also show us how we construct the world we live in.

In *Writing for Your Life*, Deena Metzger says: "Recently I added a category [of lists]: lists of lists to be made. . . . Needless to say, the lists overlap. But when the same story . . . appears on several lists, the story itself is altered by the different perspective of each list."[5]

Flex-Your-Creativity Exercises

Metzger is pointing to the intelligence behind the way a list is sorted because the list itself—the order revealed by slicing through reality in one specific direction—influences how we see the listed items individually and how they appear in the whole array.

I was drawn to this idea of making lists of lists. Instead of a list of ordinary items, this opens your list to more abstract items. In a list like the ones Metzger is encouraging us to make, each item is a possibility, something that lies in the future. Lists of lists to be made someday. When will we make these lists? Maybe when more information comes in or when we develop new ways to know things. What's critical here, and most helpful, is this exercise can force you to think in an entirely new way.

For you, the exercise is to create your own list of lists to be made. What will be on yours?

Here are some of the ways I responded to this challenge when I was working my way through Metzger's excellent book.

1. *Childhood memories.* This should be a detailed and exhaustive list of the ten most elusive memories from my childhood, the ones I've never been able to recover. What happened that day in Levittown, anyway?

Flex-Your-Creativity Exercises

2. *Great bike rides.* Over the years, bike rides tend to blend into one another. A list like this might be a way to recover memories of individual rides: the way the sun looked in summer while I was grinding up Old Railroad Grade and being passed by a fellow briskly walking his Labrador retriever. Or the day I was learning to use "clipless" pedals and glided up to a junction where bikers stopped for a drink and a chat—then slowly toppled over while everyone watched. Moments like that.

3. *Cars I've owned.* Every era of adulthood can be accessed through the transportation in use at the time. The fifteen-speed bike, the little Morris Minor that blew up on the New York State Thruway, the Volvos, always the Volvos. What might I learn from this list? Would it include that cherry Mercedes coupe, the one we put $1,000 down on before the seller turned off his telephone and disappeared, along with the money?

4. *Parallel lines.* Okay, I admit this seems a little odd. But from where I sit, the orderly rows of boxwood hedges, the sidewalk running next to the curb, the trail winding through the thicket of oaks above Point San Pedro—each has something to teach

Flex-Your-Creativity Exercises

me, something it wants to say. And a list is the way to get to that.

5. *People whose names match their occupations.* These are sometimes called "aptronyms." Remember Margaret Spellings, George W. Bush's secretary of education? What about professional golfer Andrew Parr? Wouldn't that be a great list? A kind of tail wagging the dog. There's Richard Seed, a pioneer of reproductive technology, and American cognitive psychologist Professor Martin Braine. It just goes on and on.

6. *Things I hate to do.* Don't you think we're defined just as much by the things we hate as by the things we love? But who spends time tracking these? I find it much easier to say which things I hate. If you ask me what I really love, I become a babbling idiot. But what do I hate? Don't get me started.

There's a power simply in the act of naming and describing some of these lists. They allow you to detach your mind from the trivia usually involved in the making of lists while unleashing the organizing power of a list on a whole host of other issues—any issues you want, in fact. There are lists to be made; better get started!

Flex-Your-Creativity Exercises

∴ WRITE A HAIKU ∴

For writers, *constraining* our writing by voluntarily adapting limits of some kind often forces us into a creative mind-set we might not otherwise have reached. We do this, for instance, in freewriting, where we write continuously and quickly and for a set amount of time. These constraints can profoundly change our relationship to our creative source.

Any constraint can potentially work to inspire you. Try writing in iambic pentameter for a while. It's quite challenging but also refreshing. (See chapter 24 for an example.)

For a great way to explore constraints and how they can stimulate your creative output, I've found nothing is better than writing in the Japanese poetry form called "haiku."

A haiku consists of three lines, and each line has a required number of syllables adding up to seventeen:

First line, five syllables
Second line, seven syllables
Last line, five syllables

Flex-Your-Creativity Exercises

This is a strict form to follow. You can't rant, you can't develop a character, and you can't tell a funny dentist joke.

You've got only three lines.

Here's an example to inspire you from Murakami Kijo, a haiku master who lived from 1865 to 1938:

> First autumn morning:
> the mirror I stare into
> shows my father's face.

Haiku is considerably more subtle and involved than the simple five-seven-five syllable count, and if this interests you, I encourage you to pursue this form of poetry because it is rich with creative potential. Classical haiku involves more requirements, but even keeping yourself to this simple five-seven-five form and focusing on nature and the juxtaposition of unlike elements can spur your own creativity.

Flex-Your-Creativity Exercises

∴ TAKE A WALK ∴

One of the best ways to stimulate your creativity is to move out of your usual spot behind a desk or at your computer to a completely different place.

Taking a walk somewhere that I'm exposed to more of the natural world works best for me. It's quite meditative and releases thoughts ordinarily buried under the weight of my day-to-day concerns.

Even if you don't have a nature trail or park nearby, try to get outside even for a few minutes. It will help clear your mind, getting it ready for new things to enter.

But walking is the best. Maybe the rhythmic nature of walking, where we tend to fall into a comfortable stride, gets the brain moving. Maybe it's the fresh air.

Whatever it is, I know of no better way to clear out the cobwebs and open one to new insights. A long walk can also provide time for "long thoughts," the ones usually interrupted by phone calls, needy pets, schedules, and the demands of friends, family, and colleagues.

Some of the great aspects of this exercise are it doesn't cost anything but your time, you can do it almost anywhere, and no special equipment is required.

Flex-Your-Creativity Exercises

If you're collaborating with someone on a project, arrange to go walking together. You never know what may arise to reward you for taking this initiative.

A few years ago, recovering from surgery, I was encouraged to walk as often as I could. In the beginning, on some days I could barely manage to walk, very slowly, once or twice around my backyard. That was it.

But the virtue of walking so slowly soon revealed itself: I could see so much more of the details, patterns, colors, and layout of the yard and the various flowers, bushes, trees, and landscaping there than I usually notice. It created an appreciation for a part of my home I rarely spent much time looking at and inspired new connections in my writing.

This is time you take for yourself, and that makes it important. Set a reminder or an alarm to jolt you during the rush of your ordinary days to remember to take this time, even if it's only five or ten minutes, to recharge and refresh your mental state. It will pay you back handsomely.

Flex-Your-Creativity Exercises

∴ DAILY CREATIVE PRACTICE ∴

Nothing will reward you more in your quest to improve your craft than establishing a daily creative practice. Your commitment to your daily practice will provide the framework you need to work regularly on your writing, composing, drawing, or whatever art you practice.

Here are some tips on creating your own daily practice:

- *Determine when your creative output is at its best.* Many writers use mornings, when the hubbub of the day hasn't gotten started yet, to write. I've used mornings for many years as the time I do most of my creative work. Other writers prefer the late hours, when things calm down again. Consistently use whatever time works best for you. The subtle force of this routine will help you stick to your daily goal.
- *Do your practice at the same time in the same place every day, no matter how small your output is for any particular day.* The cues you receive from your environment will help you drop into the creative flow, even when you think you're not particularly creative.

Flex-Your-Creativity Exercises

- *Establish a ritual if it helps you.* Get a cup of tea; use your favorite mug; put on music that eases you into a creative flow. These actions can help you get started and will shift you into a creative space on off days.
- *Find an environment that works for you.* Some people like perfect quiet. I took a cue from chess prodigy Bobby Fischer, who supposedly would go to a construction site in Manhattan with his portable chess set to practice. Using distraction like this forces you to focus on your task, and it can be surprisingly effective. For me, coffee shops or other public places have just the right level of distraction, and they're where I do a lot of my most productive work.

Take the time to create your own daily creative practice. Days add up rather quickly, and you'll be amazed at how much work you can get done incrementally and how your craft improves from regular exercise.

Flex-Your-Creativity Exercises

∴ HARNESS YOUR MOODS ∴

Throughout this book, I've encouraged you to establish a daily practice for yourself and then to show up for it as regularly as you can. This is a commitment you make to yourself and your work that will pay dividends forever.

But another aspect of writing or other creative pursuits relies more on the day-to-day disruptions to our equanimity. Consider this: do you write, play, or create when you're depressed or when you're anxious and worried about something in the future? How about when you've had a disturbing interaction with someone and your insides are churning?

Many people turn to their expressive work in situations like these, and that's a boon of its own. Works created in the throes of grief or melancholy or triumph embody the creator's moods in various ways.

American novelist Norman Mailer reportedly had a practice of reviewing and editing his writing in different circumstances. For example, something written when sober might come in for a rewrite when Mailer was inebriated or after he had just had a fight with someone. Maybe this was his way of incorporating many sides

Flex-Your-Creativity Exercises

of himself in his writing or arriving at a more rounded viewpoint in his books.

You can write to work out emotional issues, to raise yourself from the depths of depression, or to marvel at a moment that transported you. At first, you may need to remind yourself about this practice because when we're having strong emotions we may not think about sitting down to write. Harnessing these moods can produce some of your most powerful works.

Work on them again during your daily practice time. How do they read now? You'll be able to figure out if they have a place in your larger body of work when you review them in the "light of the day" once the emotional storm has passed.

Emotions power our writing. Finding a way to harness the emotions we all experience can give us a potent source of authentic writing, one that can be developed for years to come.

Flex-Your-Creativity Exercises

∴ BRAINSTORM: MIND MAPPING ∴

Mind mapping is a tool that allows you to visually explore and develop ideas of all kinds while avoiding the restricting structures of tools like outlining. Mind mapping is fluid, elastic, and connective, with just enough structure to allow us to establish associations and hierarchies with ease.

What does a mind map look like? How do you create one? iMindMap.com explains it this way:

> In a Mind Map, information is structured in a way that mirrors exactly how the brain functions—in a radiant rather than linear manner. A Mind Map literally "maps" out your thoughts, using associations, connections and triggers to stimulate further ideas. [Mind Maps] extract your ideas from your head into something visible and structured.

While great software is available to help you build mind maps, you can also create them with a pen and paper quite easily. The advantage of using software is the flexibility it gives you to rearrange and restructure your mind map quickly and easily.

Let's walk through a mind map so you can see exactly how this exercise works.

Flex-Your-Creativity Exercises

First, start with the subject you want to explore, an idea for a new piece of work, or anything else. I've used mind maps to plan books, presentations, and product and website launches or to plot out processes that happen in a series of steps. Really, there's no limit.

If I was going to write a memoir, it might start like this.

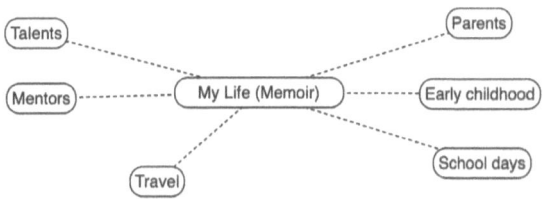

Simple, right?

Next, as subjects come to mind, I'll add them to my mind map.

Already this is helping me think about how to organize my memoir. Each subject brings up associated ideas, which I can easily start adding to the mind map.

Flex-Your-Creativity Exercises

As I go along, the mind map gives me room to add more abstract ideas and relate them to the whole. I love how fluid this process is in practice.

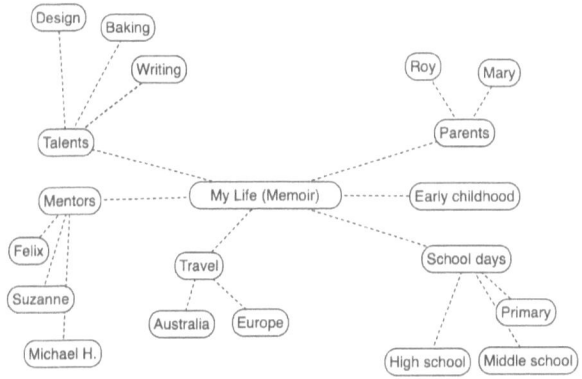

Eventually, you'll end up with a pretty big map, so you may want to split off some branches into mind maps of their own. The larger map will also start to reveal relationships you might or might not have focused on before.

This is about the simplest form of mind mapping: it requires only pen and paper. But that doesn't mean you can't elaborate, illustrate, or otherwise decorate your mind map. For example, some mind maps I've done are

Flex-Your-Creativity Exercises

quite vibrant, with colors connecting key concepts and relationships and hierarchies clearly spelled out.

Try creating your own mind map. Use these samples if you need them to get you started. You may find, as I have, that you reach for your mind mapping tools at the very beginning of a project because it's the fastest way to start exploring your subject. And because mind mapping mirrors the way our brains work, it allows you to create connections between items in a direct and visual way.

Flex-Your-Creativity Exercises

∷ WRITE A LETTER TO THE MUSE ∷

Sometimes you just get stuck on a project, and it's hard to know where to turn for advice. Here's a terrific way to get advice from a source you may not have thought of before: the muse. You may or may not have contacted your personal muse, as I described in chapter 22, but you can still make use of the magic at the center of this exercise.

If you don't have a clear picture of your muse already, see if your mind produces an image when you think of the kind of help a muse could offer you: direction for your work, answers to a specific question, discrimination or encouragement about your overall progress. In the end, the image or embodiment of the muse isn't all that important. What makes this exercise work is your willingness to ask for help.

The exercise has two parts, both of which are effective at moving you to a fresh point of view:

1. *Write a letter to the muse asking for advice.* Explain as clearly as you can where you're stuck. Be specific about the kind of advice that would be most helpful to you while acknowledging that a muse is an entity who is not under your control, who

Flex-Your-Creativity Exercises

may or may not address your questions directly. In other words, write your letter but be prepared for responses that might take any form at all.

2. *Write a letter from the muse.* Now, freewrite an answer from the muse. How will she respond? It might be with concrete suggestions, it might be with a dismissive tone, it might be with a subtle tip that doesn't appear to make sense at first.

Even though we write these letters ourselves, we don't really have much input into their content. If you can successfully contact your own stream of creativity—the entire subject of this book—you will receive feedback that can be powerful for your project or your life as a creative.

Trust the muse; she has your best interests at heart. And write often. This is a rich vein of advice and inspiration that you can tap as needed.

Notes

Chapter 3

1. "8 Rejection Letters Publishers Sent to Famous Authors," ClickHole, September 18, 2015, http://www.clickhole.com/article/8-rejection-letters-publishers-sent-famous-authors-3084.
2. "A Rejection Letter," website of Ursula K. Le Guin, June 21, 1968, http://www.ursulakleguin.com/Reject.html.

Chapter 16

3. Rilke to Andreas-Salomé, Wiesbaden, February 11, 1922, in Rainer Maria Rilke and Lou Andreas-Salomé, *Briefwechsel* (Wiesbaden, Insel Verlag, 1952), 464.

Chapter 20

4. R. S. Mollison-Read, "3 Ways in Which Music Can Inspire Writing," blog, January 6, 2014, http://rsmollisonread com/3-ways-in-which-music-can-inspire-writing/.

Flex-Your-Creativity Exercises

5. Deena Metzger, *Writing for Your Life: A Guide and Companion to the Inner Worlds* (San Francisco: HarperSanFrancisco, 1992), 62.

About the Author

JOEL FRIEDLANDER was an award-winning book designer, blogger, and writer and the author of *Body Types: The Enneagram of Essence Types; A Self-Publisher's Companion; The Book Blueprint;* and coauthor of *The Self-Publisher's Ultimate Resource Guide.*

He was a columnist for *Publishers Weekly,* and *Writer's Digest* had named him as one of the ten people to follow in book publishing.

Joel was the founder of TheBookDesigner, a popular blog on book design, book marketing, and the future of the book, and operated numerous e-commerce sites based on his creative output.

www.ingramcontent.com/pod-product-compliance
Lightning Source LLC
Chambersburg PA
CBHW030529010526
44110CB00048B/872